Clairvoyant Investigations

1 *The Archangel Bethelda, Western England. This angelic being's communication with Geoffrey Hodson is described in the introduction to his book* The Kingdom of the Gods *and in* The Brotherhood of Angels and Men.

Clairvoyant Investigations

By Geoffrey Hodson

*This publication made possible with
the assistance of the Kern Foundation*

THE THEOSOPHICAL PUBLISHING HOUSE
Wheaton, Ill. U.S.A. / Madras, India / London, England

The Theosophical Publishing House
306 West Geneva Road
Wheaton, Illinois 60189
Published by the Theosophical Publishing House,
a department of the Theosophical Society in America.

Library of Congress Cataloging in Publication Data

Hodson, Geoffrey.
  Clairvoyant investigations.

  "A Quest original"—Verso of t.p.
  Includes bibliographical references.
    1. Clairvoyance.   2. Angels—Miscellanea.   3. Music—
Miscellanea.   I. Title.
BF1325.H58   1984   299'.934   84-40166
ISBN 0-8356-0585-X (pbk.)

Printed in the United States of America

Contents

Illustrations

Other books by Geoffrey Hodson

The Brotherhood of Angels and Men
The Call to the Heights
The Christ Life from Nativity to Ascension
Fairies at Work and Play
Hidden Wisdom in the Holy Bible, Volumes I through IV
The Kingdom of the Gods
The Miracle of Birth
Music Forms
Reincarnation: Fact or Fallacy?

Cover design by William Dichtl

Foreword

"One day as, on a hillside at the edge of a beech forest in a secluded valley in the West of England, I was seeking ardently to enter the Sanctuary of Nature's hidden life, for me the heavens suddenly became filled with light." So wrote Geoffrey Hodson in 1952, introducing his magnificent work, *The Kingdom of the Gods*. The experience to which he referred had taken place many years previously, but his description of it in retrospect contained the essence of his life-long commitment to that quest for understanding which is the heart of the theosophical path to knowledge. "Seeking ardently"—that whole-hearted and one-pointed determination to pierce the veil of appearances, to discover the truth whatever the cost— this was the key to Mr. Hodson's life and work.

For above all, the late Mr. Hodson was a student and a researcher, endeavoring always to investigate, to probe, to understand; and with that profound humility characteristic of the genuine student, he constantly said: "As I see it . . .," "So far as my limited knowledge enables me to say . . .," and "Thus have I heard . . . ." Yet his search and study were centered in a profound conviction of the unitary nature of all existence. The concept of an "Absolute, Unknowable, Infinite and Unchanging Source and Foundation," to use his own words, was no mere theory to him, but a conviction deeply rooted in his own perception of life. His intuitive vision of an Ultimate Reality was always grounded in a logic derived from his own clairvoyant investigations. What is more, he willingly submitted the fruit of those investigations to analysis by others, eager to be certain that his observations were valid insofar as confirmation could be secured, either through comparison of his findings with those of other trained clairvoyants or through such other means as might be utilized.

Although he was one of the finest exponents of the theosophical philosophy which the Theosophical Society has ever known, Mr. Hodson's unique contributions were undoubtedly in the field of clairvoyant research, particularly in those areas presented in this present volume—(a) the forms produced in subtle matter as a result of various types of music, and (b) the appearance and nature of the entire range of those intelligences known as the angelic hosts, from the lowliest of nature spirits to the mightiest of those creative powers which aid in building and guiding the universal processes through all the cycles of manifested existence. It must be emphasized, however, that all of these researches into the realms of the invisible (to physical sight), into the "sanctuary of nature's hidden life," were carried forward, not simply because Mr. Hodson possessed a natural clairvoyance which was sharpened through disciplined training, but more importantly because it was his deepest conviction that neglect of the teachings of the Arcane Wisdom, including lack of understanding of the *living* quality of nature, could only result in disastrous consequences for all life on this planet. To understand, therefore, the urgent need for man to know the seamless fabric of reality underlying all phenomena, to recognize the unitary nature of life itself however diverse its forms, and to cooperate with the one Divine Plan, was the message contained in all of Mr. Hodson's work. Through lectures to large audiences throughout the world, through numerous books and articles, in personal and private letters to his incredibly large number of correspondents, he virtually pleaded with all earnest seekers to take up that work: to serve humanity and life itself through a direct knowledge that there is but "One Presence and Power within which all things live and move and have their being." We must use all our faculties, he would say repeatedly, to heal the world's ills, to prevent nuclear holocaust, to save humanity from its own misguided (because of ignorance) and mistaken actions that could only lead it down the road to further tragedy and ultimate destruction.

Having seen that light which filled the heavens, as he recorded in relating the memory of his early experience in contacting the angelic hosts, Mr. Hodson gave his life in service to that light in the confident faith that the darkness of ignorance could indeed be dispelled. For those who knew him, he was the most selfless of individuals. His gifts, and they were many, were used always in the service of others and in the service of the One. Paradox it may be for those who do not yet know the truth of the theosophic vision, but for Mr. Hodson there was no distinction between "others" and "the One." In serving others, he served the One; in serving the One radiant presence and power, he gave himself to others.

He himself stated the vision, in his preface to *The Kingdom of the Gods*:

> What then is the ultimate discovery, the Himalayan summit? At the heart of the Cosmos there is ONE. That ONE has Its

sanctuary and shrine in the heart of every human being. The first major discovery is of this Presence within. . . . Ultimately, identity with the ONE ALONE, fully conscious absorption for evermore in the eternal, self-existent ALL, is attained. *This is the goal.*

So he adventured all his life on the path to that goal; so he called all who would listen to join in that great adventure. The words of *The Voice of the Silence* were to him a living reality: "Can there be bliss when all that lives must suffer? Shalt thou be saved and hear the whole world cry?" In the light of that dual, yet single, question, Mr. Hodson was less concerned in achieving the goal than in sharing the adventures and experiences along the way, "hoping," as he said, "that they may inform and help others who similarly seek." In that spirit, he offered all his work, especially the researches and the fruition of his observations now published in this volume.

JOY MILLS, Director
Krotona School of Theosophy

Krotona
December 1983

xii

Geoffrey Hodson's Clairvoyant Research

For many years, Geoffrey Hodson has co-operated with various scientifically qualified people in attempts to demonstrate the research potential of superphysical faculties of perception, with which he is evidently highly gifted. From 1978 to 1981 I was closely associated with him as assistant and technical adviser in two such pieces of research.

The first of these was an extensive series of observations of the superphysical effects of musical sounds and pieces. The record of his descriptions of these effects is extremely interesting from the artistic, acoustic, psychosomatic and other points of view. Having been present with him for approximately 20 hour-long sessions in this and another investigation, I feel able to offer some impressions of his attitude and approach to this work.

I have been repeatedly struck by his integrity and uncompromising desire to seek the truth in every situation, regardless of any risk of possible conflict with established findings of the scientific establishment or of earlier theosophical investigators. At the same time, he is clearly aware of the difficulties and limitations inherent in any process of observation, especially one involving inner levels of the psyche, and has a tremendously careful and indeed craftsmanlike attitude to the handling and direction of his extended perceptive abilities.

In my opinion, Geoffrey Hodson has amply succeeded in his goals of (a) indicating the potential of superphysical research methods, (b) producing material of great interest to the enquiring mind and (c) providing a stimulus to others to follow his footsteps and expand and consolidate this work.

MURRAY A. STENTIFORD, M.Sc. (physics)

Wellington, New Zealand
May 1982

Acknowledgments

I wish to express my profound gratitude to the following people who assisted me in the production of Part I of this volume which chronicles my research into the angelic kingdom: my beloved wife Sandra, who took down every word of each description of Devas in longhand and finally presented this in typewritten form, as well as contributing to the work in other valued ways; Myra G. Fraser of Auckland, New Zealand, my friend and valued literary assistant who has aided me over a period of many years; Marvin Richard Gratiot of California, U.S.A., Gaile V. Campbell of Vancouver, Canada, Frank A. Eden, Angela Meeson, and Ruth Sharkey, all of Auckland, for so generously and effectively providing the illustrations.

I also wish to thank Mrs. Florence Tiddeman, a late member of the Theosophical Society, who owned a beautifully situated cottage in the English village of Shepscombe, Gloucestershire, England. In response to repeated intuitive guidance this lady offered to me tenancy of the house, to use freely as if it were my own. I wish, therefore, to express the very strong feeling of respect and gratitude which immediately developed within me and has since deepened. This is particularly true since this action on her part made possible my books on the subject of the angelic hosts, beginning with *The Brotherhood of Angels and Men* and culminating thus far in *The Kingdom of the Gods,* which was so beautifully illustrated by Ethelwynne M. Quail. In this present volume I thus wish to give full expression to my deep appreciation of the generosity of this greatly valued friend and helper.

Regarding Part II of this volume on the inner effects of music, I wish to express grateful appreciation to Mrs. Peace Thorn who took down in shorthand all my observations and typed the first drafts of each research session; Mr. Frank Eden who produced the fine oil-painted pictures; Mr. Murray Stentiford, M.Sc., for his scientific direction; the performers: Wendy Dixon Dip, Mus. (Hons.), singing and cello, Murray Stentiford, piano and clarinet, Hugh Dixon, M.Mus., F.T.C.L., L.R.S.M., trumpet, singing, and piano, Michael Dixon, horn, Rae Dixon, piano; Mrs. Lyndall Greager for literary and typing assistance; my wife Sandra for assistance with typing; Mr. Hugh Dixon for help in arranging the contents.

In addition, I wish to express my thanks to Prof. J. T. Robinson, Dr. Sc., including Palaeontology, Dr. D. D. Lyness, M.B.Ch.B., D.P.M., M.A.N.Z.C.P., and Murray Stentiford, M.Sc. (Physics) for their affirmations of confidence—after repeated tests—in the accuracy of my capacity for fully conscious clairvoyant research.

Introduction

As part of the unfoldment of the human intellect into omni-science, at a certain stage of human evolution the faculty of fully conscious, positive clairvoyance develops. This implies an extension of the normal range of visual response to include both physical rays beyond violet and, beyond those, the light of the superphysical worlds. This can be hastened by means of self-training in the science and art of the process of self-illumination called yoga in the East.

The followers of this, the oldest and greatest of the sciences, the science of the soul, aver that extension of visual and auditory power and mastery of the forces, first of one's own nature, and then of nature herself, can be deliberately and consciously achieved. Anyone, they say, who will fulfill the necessary conditions, who will obey laws as certain in their operation as those to which the chemist subscribes in his laboratory, can pierce the veil of matter which normally hides from view the eternal, spiritual realities, as the veil of day conceals the ever-shining stars. By such means can be attained direct knowledge of the forces and intelligences of nature and the faculty of cooperating with them in what is sometimes called The Great Work.

1

Proof of this assertion can alone be found in individual experiment and investigation. Though demonstration is admittedly impossible, test by personal research is not. That test I have attempted to apply, and this book is in part a record of my own findings, which corroborate the teachings of the Ancient Wisdom.

This teaching depicts the universe as consisting of seven interpenetrating worlds or planes, composed of matter in varying degrees of density. The physical and its counterpart in the etheric, which is invisible to ordinary sight, combine to form the densest. This is followed in order of refinement by the astral or emotional, the manasic or mental, which has two grades of density, form and formless, the Buddhic or intuitional, and the Atmic or spiritual, plus two others as yet beyond the range of human consciousness.[1]

I have myself confirmed that these superphysical domains contain innumerable nonphysical beings, such as angels and nature spirits, as well as a great variety of astral emanations and thought forms, including those produced by music. On levels denser than the fourth subplane of the mental plane, the tendency to assume shape preponderates over rhythm, while in the more rarefied levels rhythm as free flow of life predominates. Beings such as angels on the lower planes present more definitely to human consciousness the idea of bodily form than do those of the higher planes.

The Wisdom teaching asserts that these inner worlds are ruled by law and intelligence as sure as is visible nature. Many scientists today have been drawn towards a conclusion similar to this and to my own, namely that intelligence is at

---

1. See my book *Basic Theosophy, the Living Wisdom* (Adyar: Theosophical Publishing House, 1981).

work in every department and aspect of nature, hence the phrase "A universe which thinks." If such theory proves to be true, as the Ageless Wisdom has always taught, then not only the physically visible, tangible, and measurable phenomena of nature will be found to operate under the impulse of an inherent intelligence, but also the denizens of the etheric and superphysical levels of density of matter will, in consequence, themselves be subject to the same directive thought.

Adept scientists and initiates through the ages and their disciples have long ago made this discovery. For them not only the physical universe, but also its etheric counterpart and superphysical planes are, in their turn, all moved by divine thought. This idea is a fulfillment, or at least an acceptance, of such concept so far as the members of the as yet scientifically undiscovered kingdoms of nature are concerned.

So far as my observations and interpretations of the superphysical planes of nature have taken me, I conclude that on behalf of our planet Earth, and of everything and every creature within and upon it, there is occurring a continual process designed to produce an evolutionary quickening, in the fulfillment of which members of the angelic hierarchy purposefully and effectively participate.[2]

---

2. This introduction and Chapter 1 contain a few short excerpts from Geoffrey Hodson's book *The Kingdom of the Gods*, reprinted by kind permission of the Theosophical Publishing House, Adyar, India.—Ed.

I

Angelic Presences

The Kingdom of God

O world invisible, we view thee,
O world intangible, we touch thee,
O world unknowable, we know thee,
Inapprehensible, we clutch thee!

Does the fish soar to find the ocean,
The eagle plunge to find the air—
That we ask of the stars in motion
If they have rumour of thee there?

Not where the wheeling systems darken,
And our benumbed conceiving soars!
The drift of pinions, would we hearken,
Beats at our own clay-shuttered doors.

The angels keep their ancient places;
Turn but a stone, and start a wing!
'Tis ye, 'tis your estranged faces,
That miss the many-splendoured thing.

But (when so sad thou canst not sadder)
Cry;—and upon thy so sore loss
Shall shine the traffic of Jacob's ladder
Pitched betwixt Heaven and Charing Cross.

Yea, in the night, my Soul, my daughter,
Cry,—clinging Heaven by the hems;
And lo, Christ walking on the water
Not of Gennesareth, but Thames!

Francis Thompson

1

Angelic Hosts and the Service of Humanity

The term *Logos* as used in this book connotes a divine Being, omnipresent as the universal energizing power, indwelling life, and directing intelligence within all substance, all beings, and all things, separate from none. This Being is manifest throughout the solar system as divine law, power, wisdom, love, and truth, as beauty, justice, and order. The Logos is the manifested Deity who speaks the creative Word whereby universes spring into being and life. This spiritual parent of all beings is regarded as both immanent within and transcendent beyond his system.[1]

At the cyclic period at which the emanation of a universe is to take place, two distinct orders of existence emerge and are made objectively manifest at levels below which all are one. On the one hand, the Logos manifests as hierarchies of beings; on the other, he[2] pours out Logoic power, life, and consciousness as an unceasing stimulus to unfoldment. The

---

1. For a further discussion of Logos and Deity, see my book *The Kingdom of the Gods* (Adyar: Theosophical Publishing House, 1980), Chapter 1.
2. The masculine pronoun is used for convenience only, the divine Life itself being of dual polarity.

hierarchy of beings, while evolving in themselves, are destined to assist in two intimately related processes, namely, Logoic manifestation within and throughout a universe-to-be, and perpetual development to greater and fuller stages of consciousness and expression.

Thus, at the heart of all universes this twin divine manifestation exists as universal power, and becomes active as irresistible "insistence" upon perpetual unfoldment or evolutionary progress at every external level. This latter is the domain, as it were, of the hierarchies of archangels and of angels, and ensures the continuous fulfillment of such evolutionary progress at every stage, from life in the submineral to that of the highest spiritual plane. This is their work or Logoic mission.

Angels or in Sanskrit *Devas*, sometimes called gods, are hierarchical orders of intelligences, quite distinct from man in this solar system, but who either have been or will be men. They are regarded as omnipresent, superphysical agents of the creative will of the Logos, as directors of all natural forces, laws, and processes, solar, interplanetary, and planetary. Manifestations of the Logos or the One, they may be regarded as the active, creative intelligences and form-builders of all objective creation. From dawn to eve of Creative Day, they are ceaselessly in action as directors, rectors, designers, artists, producers, engineers, and builders, ever subservient to and expressive of the One Will, the One Substance, and the One Thought. Thus, they are ever active in the twin manifestations of the Logos. Be it ever remembered, however, that at the Source and in reality these manifestations are actually not a separate pair but are entirely identical.

Here it may perhaps usefully be suggested that when once a human being has become sufficiently endued and empowered with and by the divine principle of perpetual un-foldment to ever greater and higher states, and the practice of yoga in whatever suitable forms is undertaken, then the unchanging goal for every yogi is the realization that the Source of these twin manifestations of the Logos is at heart *only One*, or *One Alone*. Yogis may well remember that at the loftiest levels of consciousness there cannot actually exist nor even be envisioned such a concept as a pair. In Logoic awareness—the goal of every yogi—there exists but the principle of unity and its expression and "heart" as realized *Oneness*. Thereafter, for the successful yogi, as far as the capacities of the mind permit such knowledge to be gained, the result of proficiency in the practice of yoga leads to being "dissolved" therein.[3] This implies elevation of consciousness to the level at which nothing but the *One Alone* can possibly exist, even though an interior individual identity remains.

Once these two modes of Self-manifestation and evolu-tionary progress are released into objective action, every Monad, or immortal, divine spirit, destined at any period to evolve through the human kingdom begins a series of in-carnations in matter of deepening density and the experience of consciousness of increasing limitation. Having eventually entered the extreme or most material state of solidity, the process of evolution is ceaselessly at work until its conclusion when "Logos-hood" is attained by the Monad.

Devic Monads, while themselves continuing to evolve, have a mission bestowed upon them, which they accept. This mission is single through the devic hierarchy and consists of responsibility for and continual assistance or "quickening" in the procedures of evolution. The modes of rendering such

---

3. "Dissolved" as implied by the Sanskrit word *Laya* and inculcated in *Laya Yoga*.

ministration differ greatly, however. They include the accentuation throughout a universe of the sound of the creative Word, the stimulation of consciousness at all levels, and assistance in the construction of forms according to the divinely conceived Idea. These are the accepted responsibilities of the devic hierarchy as a whole. This triple function might perhaps be named "a musical office" or "Gandharvahood," and implies the projection and production of a universe according to the divine Idea or "Word." It also includes the quickening of the unfoldment of monadic manifestation or incarnation in all stages of evolutionary progress.

As is perhaps natural, human beings who are sensitive enough to become aware of the existence of the Deva kingdom at any level are likely to perceive first the Devic intelligences at work in the third of the three above procedures, namely the nature spirits and other builders of form assisting in the construction of forms according to the divinely conceived Idea. As this awareness develops, however, perception is less limited to appearances in forms, and more knowledge develops of the other two functions—the accentuation throughout a universe of the sound of the creative Word, and the stimulation of consciousness at all levels.

The student-seer and—if the word may be used appropriately—"hearer" becomes aware of more evolved members of the angelic hierarchy. This may lead to a degree of understanding which culminates in collaboration, especially where the suffering of sentient beings is to be relieved. The student and mystic then enters into a new and advanced phase of relationship with the angelic hosts, namely benediction, inspiration, and the reduction of such suffering, in healing the sick, for example. This leads to the important, almost all-important, aspect of the kinship between members of the human and angelic hierarchies, that is to say, effectual alliance between humans and angels. This includes the ever noble and ever desirable—and unfortunately, at this stage, ever needed—function of practical collaboration in the quickening of monadic evolution throughout both human and Devic hierarchies.

Knowledge for the seer, hearer, and knower can be of very great importance and helpfulness in the evolution of mankind and its individual components. This applies especially to understanding the fact of the existence of members of the devic hierarchy as actualities within the solar system and upon the earth at its superphysical levels. This hierarchy extends plane by plane from semiconscious and dawningly conscious nature spirits, through devic dwellers in the inner worlds until the most subtle of these is reached, and on to the very great archangels at the head of that hierarchy. Such is the range of angelic beings in association with this world, and such is the expanding degree of knowledge attained by the student who becomes aware of the angelic hosts—lesser, greater, and greatest—through the acceptance of teaching from others and, most important, from direct personal, vision-inspired experience. By these two means my books on this subject have been inspired and produced, providing gradually increasing information concerning the angelic hosts.

The main functions of the devic hierarchy are described in both *The Kingdom of the Gods* and elsewhere in this volume. Nevertheless, it is desirable from the points of view of intellectual advancement, of personal progress, and especially of fulfillment of the ideal of selfless service, that such knowledge steadily increases; for more seriously minded human beings may thus achieve a quickening of their evolution and more deeply dedicate their lives to the service of others, particularly those in immediate need.

11

Psychosomatic principles, discovered by orthodox physicians in this century but always known to the few—when understood and applied even by the non-physician—are part of the dual processes of spiritual and mental healing. The members of the angelic hosts associated with those human beings who thus serve in connection with the healing of the sick can be of especial value in correcting, and even removing, mental and emotional errors and undesirable states responsible for physical sicknesses.

The human servers, in their turn, function primarily at physical levels and secondarily, though most importantly, at etheric, astral, and concrete mental levels of matter. They also assist in healing the human vehicles built thereof. A broken heart, for example, with its most painful effects upon the sufferer's body, has its corresponding undesirable conditions at the superphysical levels, and these can be reduced by the angels. So, also, mental errors, disturbances, and sickness-producing habits have their associated existence in the mind-body, and with human aid they can be gradually reduced and even entirely removed, especially when members of both the human and the angelic hierarchies collaborate.

Similarly, not only broken hearts but all emotional afflictions affect the astral body of the sufferer. These, too, are susceptible of both reduction and eventual removal by the cooperation of angels and human beings. This applies particularly in the procedures used by healers who are not necessarily physicians, although the latter may also be thus aided. Therefore, not only in the fields of health and happiness but also in very many others, sincerely sought and wisely directed angelic participation in human healing from sufferings of almost every kind can be achieved most effectively.

True, the guardian at the door of such a "temple of healing" is under the dominion of that great decider of human fate named karma or karmic law, the universal law of cause and effect which assures absolute justice to every human being.[4] Nevertheless, there is virtually no state of human need, even under most rigid karmic decree, that cannot at some level or other receive beneficial ministration. Even the knowledge by sufferers that such benedictions are invoked on their behalf is helpful, if only because it reduces and may even banish pains of heart and mind primarily due to loneliness.

The human ministrant may, particularly at first, be quite unable to perceive the psychic and superphysical correspondences to physical complaints.[5] This in no sense reduces the readiness to assist and the responses of orders of healing angels to whom, perchance, the psychic disorders appear nearer to the root causes of suffering than the actual physical ones.

Those who know and understand the fact of the existence and function of the angelic hosts, and still more so the clairvoyant "seers," are able more directly to participate in superphysical healing with angelic aid than those not as yet so endowed. This knowledge need not, however, be dependent upon clairvoyance alone, for while thoroughly tested and completely proven clairvoyant vision can be of great value, it is by no means a necessity in the service of one's fellow men in every walk of life and in every psychological condition. Knowledge intuitively responded to is virtually of equal

---

4. See my book *Reincarnation, Fact or Fallacy?* (Adyar: Theosophical Publishing House, 1970), especially the chapter "Reincarnation."
5. See my book *Basic Theosophy, the Living Wisdom,* especially the chapter "Man's Cosmic Powers."

value and can be just as convincing and as effective, for the actual superphysical needs and procedures of healing are directly seen and treated by collaborating healing angels; hence again, the importance of such cooperation. Ideal healers of every human ill are therefore those who, by study and naturally favorable responses, are able more and more consciously to invoke and to collaborate with members of the healing orders of angels; hence information on this subject is here proffered.

There also exists the all-important ministration by the selfless servants of humanity of saving individuals, groups, and even nations from moving towards tragedy and downfall— dangers that unfortunately exist in calamitous degrees. Here the true and so most effective "medication" is knowledge, and the acceptance of guidance based thereon—further reasons for the presentation by great adepts of information (*Theosophia*) concerning the nature of man and the purpose of his existence. Unhappily, although continuously provided from remotest times, such guidance in the past has not been and is not even now sufficiently heeded. The misled and selfishly motivated "sick" have been, however, and fortunately still can be "saved" by the wisely and acceptably proffered teachings of the Ancient Wisdom. These include information on the nature and purpose of life on this planet, and on the existence of angelic beings, and such knowledge can be of almost immeasurable help to those on the threshold of downfall and even to those who have already fallen; hence, again, this proffered information.

2

Hephaestus

The Greek God of Fire

Homer and other authors generated the quite fascinating "fairy tale" of the existence and experiences of the divine Blacksmith, Hephaestus. The fairy tale, if with certain exceptions it may be so regarded, is an enchanting and even humorous story, although parts of it are quite tragic. However, some references in Greek mythology may indicate that the authors were inspired by one or other of the seven Greek sages.

Hephaestus' mastery over metals and his ability, not only to forge armor and other metallic objects, but also to create living beings (such as his handmaidens and Pandora with her box, which she so tragically opened) demonstrate highly occult powers. These achievements, I suggest, may possibly be interpreted as referring to the fundamental processes of the evolution of the indwelling spiritual life from the mineral kingdom, through the plant and animal kingdoms, and on into the human kingdom and beyond as represented by elevation to immortal life on Mt. Olympus. The fact that Hephaestus was the offspring of Zeus, the Father of gods and men, the supreme ruler of Olympus, and Hera his wife, or perchance of Hera alone, may refer to the source of his being

15

and also to his evolution through the Deva and Devaraja stages of consciousness and attainments; for, of course, the Deva kingdom is a radiation from and an "offspring" of the Supreme Deity.[1]

If this concept be acceptable, then the capacity to make gross metals so malleable that they could be hammered and molded into desired shapes, even of great beauty, and still more to bring out of the metal gold, as it were, actual living human beings, indicates the ability to intrude effectively upon the life and consciousness in those kingdoms of nature. This would include the power miraculously to bring the life incarnate in gross mineral substances such as lead, iron, and rock, eventually into living human beings, thus indicating the capability to aid in the evolution of that hidden life.

The student of occult science may at once be reminded of that function of a certain order of Devas which is intimately associated with the evolution of life in form, such order being engaged, throughout the period of a manifested world in quickening evolutionary progress. This is accompanied by the hastening of the process of freeing life from imprisonment in one kingdom—the mineral, for example—and its absorption into the composite materials of which the human body is built. Thus regarded, Hephaestus personifies that order of Devas among many others, to which this task has been committed, namely to stimulate evolutionary development and so hasten advancement from one kingdom of nature to its successor. My attempted exploration of the kingdom of the gods, and even some association with members of the angelic hosts, have revealed to me that this Hephaestus-like labor is the function of certain of the members of the Devic hierarchy.

---

1. See my book, *The Concealed Wisdom in World Mythology* (Adyar: Theosophical Publishing House, 1983).

The fact that for untold ages these beings must deal with the substances of the planet Earth itself, especially minerals and plants, supports this conclusion. Such "limitation" is hinted at by the casting of Hephaestus out of heaven, his ugliness and his lameness, these being only symbols, I suggest, of the apparently accepted restrictions.

In *The Kingdom of the Gods* I have described "gods" who have been thus engaged, some of them portrayed in certain of the illustrations as being in the midst of such activities—the mountain gods, for example, as also the tree Devas. Furthermore, the whole hierarchy of the Gandharvas, the angels of music who perpetually sound forth and re-sound the uttered creative "Word" from within the formless levels of nature, may—and, I feel sure, do—continually exert an evolution-assisting influence upon the life in all nature and within the inner selves of human beings.[2]

By the "pouring" of the Kundalini Fire-Shakti (occult electricity or supersensuous spiritual essence) into the sleeping life of minerals, this life is rendered more responsive to the general outpouring and inpouring of evolution-quickening power, which landscape Devas throughout the world infuse into both its mineral and plant life.[3] The downward energy is, as it were, also impressed, indoctrinated, or infiltrated with and made to vibrate at the frequencies of the divine thought of the molecular combinations and of the ultimate forms and shapes in the plant kingdom. The outpoured and inpoured forces which the Devas "inject" into the planet's mineral and plant kingdoms thus perform a dual function. One of these is to quicken the evolution of the

---

2. Gandharvas. *The Kingdom of the Gods*, pp. 231, 232.
3. Ibid. Plates 9, 12, and 17.

indwelling life. The other is to render it more responsive to divine, formative thought, thereby increasing the permeation therewith, the effect of which is to cause material substances more and more readily to produce the planet's myriad forms according to the divine thought or Logoic Word.

This dual ministration—evolution-quickening and form-producing—is represented in the Hephaestus story by the forge, with its indwelling and its associated substances becoming increasingly responsive to the divine Idea. Similarly, by melting and so softening a metal such as iron, the metal is rendered more responsive to the shaping process performed on the anvil by the hammers, according to the design in the blacksmith's mind. The other function is as described—a continuous quickening of the evolutionary processes within the life incarnate in all mineral, plant, aerial, and fluid substances.

The fact that the armor and implements produced in the forge of Hephaestus were all, or nearly all, made for and donated to either heroes or half-gods, indicates that divine and "semidivine" procedures in nature are being rendered increasingly and more rapidly effective than normal. This is typical of the devic power to quicken the indwelling life in all nature, thereby causing it to be more responsive to the divine will-thought than would otherwise be the case.

3

A Kundalini Deva

Urquhart's Bay, Onerahi, Whangarei, New Zealand

Far down in the core of the earth, Kundalini, the power of life, arises from a great fire, perhaps in the center of the planet, and a caduceus-like stream flows up in concentrated form through the whole mountain, shooting high up into the air, probably for one thousand feet. In the midst of this stream, above the summit, is to be seen the great Deva through and within which arises the specialized and localized triple current—Ida (feminine), Pingala (masculine), and Sushumna (neutral).[1]

The lower aura of the Deva opens out downwards for several hundred feet like an inverted and widening cup. [2] The current itself then reaches the place where the "body" would be and concentrates into the triple Kundalini. This fiery current moves up through the center of the "body," the Sushumna rising out of the "head" of the Deva with Ida to the left (the ocean beach side) and Pingala to the right (Urquhart's Bay side), but all ascending together and widening out as they do so.

---

1. See *Kingdom of the Gods*, pp. 238-41.

19

From heights above the Deva and downwards through the aura,[2] but not in the central area, streams a tremendous descent of the life-stimulating power for which the Deva is also an agent. There is thus an almost pillar-shaped upward movement *within* the Deva and a downward movement from high above in a continually widening stream, like an inverted funnel, reaching over half a mile into the rock beneath if not more.

The central *chakras,* or vortical force centers which convey life-force between planes,[3] lie in their normal relatively human positions and glow, strangely, not only in one direction, but at least forwards towards us and backwards and to both sides as well. Each chakram is therefore fourfold with, of course, a central source.

I receive the impression that the Kundalini power is inwardly drawn up and concentrated around the form constituting—if one may use the word—the soul of the Deva, with the radiating, outflowing forces forming the aura. The height of the central form is at least three times that of the bare, rock-like summit where the vegetation ends, possibly much more.

2. Angels as well as humans display an aura of subtle, invisible, super-physical essence at the etheric, astral, and/or mental levels. See C. W. Leadbeater, *Man Visible and Invisible* (Wheaton, IL: Theosophical Publishing House, 1980).—ED.

3. See C. W. Leadbetter, *The Chakras* (Wheaton, IL: Theosophical Publishing House, 1980).

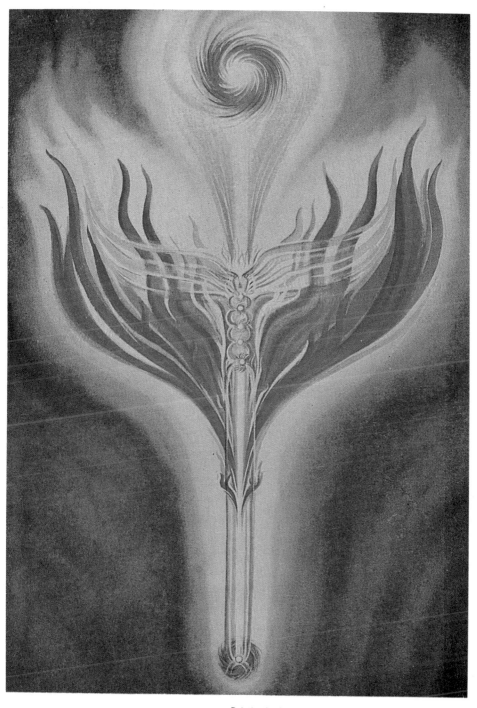

Painting by Ethelwynne Quail, reprinted by kind permission
of the Theosophical Publishing House, Adyar.

2 *A Kundalini Deva, Urquhart's Bay, Onerahi, Whangarei, New Zealand*

4

An Archangel of Creative Light

Onerahi, Whangarei, North Auckland

During a vacation at Onerahi some hundred miles north of Auckland, New Zealand, my wife Sandra and I were reflecting together one morning upon the subject of the hierarchy of the Devas of this planet and their functions in the processes of nature. Suddenly there appeared in the sky beyond our hotel window a number of great and brilliantly shining Devas. One of these approached us more closely and flashed the following communication into my mind: "With yourself, we members of the devic hierarchy are veritable manifestations of the great procedures of external creation emanating from the most deeply interior Source of the outwardly 'knowable,' objectively existent universe, all nature at every level."

Never before do I remember having perceived so great a being. It is describable, within my limits, only as an individualized archangelic center of creative light. Shining forth from and through the angel, as if from star-shaped centers of force, were radiations of form-producing ideas, forces, and light. This Devaraja would seem to be carrying out individually—but with cosmically expanded consciousness—the procedures of the formation and preservation of the universe. Some of the white, five-pointed, four-dimensional stars were apparently permanent in the upper portion of the extensively shining aura. Yet, strangely, they also appeared to be constantly flashing forth and transmitting their light, thereafter disappearing as if the source of the light had completed its manifestation. This continued throughout the upper portion of the aura, not only at the front but also at the sides and behind the great and shining being.

The predominating color of the lower half of the aura, which spread downwards from a region corresponding to the solar plexus in man, was leaf-green with touches of gold and white, somewhat like rays shining within it. Wing-like radiations, sky-blue and gold in color, shone above the "shoulders" high into the air. The "eyes" were more like great centers of light than our human organs, of course, and the color gold was seen to be glowing both within the "head" and radiating upwards beyond. The auric activity of this great being was definitely wing-like and wing-shaped.

5

A Devaraja of Planetary Power

Lion Rock, McLeod's Bay, Whangarei Heads

The auric form and center of consciousness or "head" of this Deva are far above the physical rocks. [3] The great, even huge, downward sweep of the lower part of the aura covers the whole threefold mountain. The predominating colors are radiating purple light with bright grass-green to the left, or seawards. White streams of force are pouring down in relatively narrow streams within and without the central "form," almost but not quite producing a folded or even pleated effect.

A white, evolution-quickening force is being "driven" through the lower aura and far down into the rock beneath, actually reaching below the level of the water and descending to about half the height of the mountain. A tremendous amount of stimulation and intellectually directed activity is most obviously taking place, with an intensity almost beyond human conception, as if performed by a superhuman being operating with the greatest possible power. This rock-enfolding, down-pouring, and out-spreading stream of spiritualizing energies reaches below the mountain into the water of the harbor, outwards to the sea, and inland to the surrounding landscape.

24

Painting by Marvin Richard Gratiot

3 *The Deva of Lion Rock, McLeod's Bay, Whangarei Heads, North Auckland*

In addition, from the area where in a human form shoulders would be, and across the central form of the triple peak of Lion Rock, another stream of blue power is being propelled vertically into the ground, mingling there with the purple and white projected forces previously described. The position of the Deva's "head" suggests a location, so far as physical measurements could apply, about three times higher than the right-hand rock. The aura in front of and even within the regions of the "face" and "neck" and towards the "heart" is purple in color, with lighted edges of an indefinite but discernible shape resembling a human head, neck, shoulders, and heart. From this latter there streams forth what at this first study appears to be a fourfold, cross-like outpouring in all directions at the "heart" level, far beyond my psychic range of vision, and resembling a tremendous lighthouse raying outwards four great beams of power. The "throat" area shines with the same grass-green light before mentioned, and the region of the foci of forces at the position of the "eyes" is some six or more inches in diameter.

The center of consciousness is established at the position where the "head" would be. Radiations of an apparently more refined and even more delicate type of power are streaming outwards from the whole region of the "head" and beyond for a distance, some six times its width. At a higher level there is a magnificent uprush of white, golden and purple colors reaching far beyond my range. While this phenomenon continues, "explosions" of white-gold power appear to be occurring within it, producing a magnificent fiery, bejewelled crown, above which streams of force vertically radiate.

Contacted at a higher condition of consciousness—Atma, Buddhi, Manas—the Devaraja is more clearly perceived. Here, strangely enough, the sense of individuality is very marked, and one perceives the inmost "Selfhood" of this truly glorious being, the chief colors seeming to be largely white with blended purple and topaz-like shadings.

This great being, I must assume, is a purely First Ray Devaraja,[1] which has held its position at the Whangarei Heads at least since Atlantean days. Hence my impression that the evolution-quickening, downward radiations reach far into the earth beneath the waters of the harbor. The same is true of a large area of submerged land from the seashore outwards including the islands and for a considerable distance beyond, even to some fifty miles from the rock itself. Hosts of co-operative Devas, down to the level of highly evolved sylphs, are at work within these streams of Deva-directed power, and also within the aura of the Lion Rock Devaraja. All of the members of the devic hierarchy are themselves being quickened in evolution, while at the same time acquiring and practicing added faculties, thereby more effectively assisting in the conveyance of the evolutionary forces into the land beneath.

While observing this great Deva, I am impressed by its condition of consciousness, which is dispassionate, utterly withdrawn from anything but the major planetary function upon which it is engaged. Unlike the other Devas investigated, my attempted study evokes no slightest response. Indeed, the center of awareness is, I presume, entirely Atmic, at which highest spiritual level I now see the extraordinary phenomenon of the lateral shining forth of a pure white power in the four main directions—one out to sea, one inland, and the other two at right angles on either side. At the center is the purely Atmic or spiritual identity, the other radiations con-

---

1. The seven Rays indicate the powers and qualities of seven different temperaments, First Ray being the kingly Ray of leadership and will power.—ED.

27

sisting of the "core" of the three vehicles—Atmic, Buddhic and Manasic—from which, as described, partially scintillate all the numerous brilliantly glowing streams of energy. Each of these shines as if lighted from within, the chief colors being purple and green shot through with white. This outpouring does not consist entirely of single, unbroken, ever-flowing currents, but also includes an effect which would be caused by minor interruptions, each one conveying deeply and in highly concentrated form evolution-stimulating and life-quickening successive "notes," to use a musical term.

Purple is the predominating color of the lower aura. Curiously, if I am correct, where the "body" would be in a human form—namely, from the level of the neck and shoulders downwards almost to the surface of the ground—the formation is *not* funnel-shaped but almost geometrically quadrilateral or four-sided, and tremendously powerful. This immovable core or base stabilizes the whole "mechanical" structure and is an extension in the form-worlds of the adopted "body" of the great being that reaches almost down to the level of the lower astral plane near the physical level. The "shoulders" themselves would be at a height about equal to that of the tallest rock above the surface of the water.

Again, I discern an expression of absolutely detached stillness, impersonal to the last degree, and appearing to be, but possibly not entirely, irrevocably stern or rock-like. The same applies, may I say in all humility, to the mighty intelligence, the Mahadevaraja of the North Island of New Zealand whose awareness seems to be deeply focused inwards in realized unity and identity with the nameless One Source of All.[2] At these levels, I presume, there exists what might perhaps be described as *stillness absolute*, a rock-like firmness doubtless

2. See Chapter 8.

28

Painting by Marvin Richard Gratiot

4 *The Deva of Lion Rock—a second view*

developed throughout vast ages as a manifestation of the one Supreme Existence.

Further research verifies my previous findings with regard to the Mahadevaraja of the North Island. [4] I now perceive this detachment and stillness to be necessary for both inward perception and outward direction of forces. Just as an electric machine is built of steel and is in itself motionless, even though movement is occurring within and beyond it, so also this wondrous being might be reverently regarded not inappropriately as a devic electric power generator and distributor, like an immense source of the indwelling life-consciousness of nature, an evolutionary stimulant. Green and slate grey, with flashes and areas of gold, are the colors of this devic "generating station."

The whole aura radiates as far as half a mile from Mt. Manaia, Whangarei Heads, and for some three-quarters of a mile all around Mt. Aubrey. It consists also of tremendously potent outpoured streams or lines of auric power. Parts of the aura penetrate Mt. Manaia quite deeply. In addition, from the "shoulders" of the Deva a widening uprush of auric forces is occurring, these being chiefly green and gold with light yellow at the top, and there is a tremendous chakram of many hues positioned at the "throat." This is twofold, facing both forwards and backwards, and is concerned both with the reception from still higher planes—Atma at least—and with the transmission of power supplied from those lofty planetary levels and even from solar systemic ones, I am moved to conclude.

Hosts of as yet unindividualized sylphs are moving constantly within and through this outpoured energy from all directions, but chiefly from the "shoulders" and sides of the "head." The consciousness of this great Deva impresses me

tremendously, being almost everlastingly established in stillness, immovable and undisturbable, thereby ensuring the
tremendous power reception and power transmission for
which in this area it is responsible. I am disposed to believe
that it holds an extremely important, almost planetary, position and thus fulfills an energy-directing office for this our
earth. This great being performs for the planet the same functions as other devic agents which are established as recipients
and transmitters of power throughout the surface of the
globe. The Deva of the South African Karoo Desert, I remember, is another such,[3] while at the North and South
Poles tremendous concentrations of Mahadevic power have
their radiation centers.

Thus the whole globe is "kept in balance" in some mysterious way beyond my knowledge. It was this as a principle
which I glimpsed as a form, taking the apparent shape of the
six-pointed star. With added contact and knowledge, and
especially the understanding now gained, I see that I was
blending the principle of planetary-balancing power with
clairvoyantly visible devic aura-forms. I now perceive that—
except as an active principle at work in the Manasic-Atmic
being and aura of the Devaraja—no such actual mento-astral
form is visible. At the higher mental level where principles
reside I was correct, but at astral levels not actually so.

I venture to say that I am also conscious of an associated
Devi,[4] in which the feminine divine principle is manifest, at a
lofty spiritual plane. This being is a marvelously shining, dif-
ferently crowned collaborator. The crown consists primarily
of a ring of flashing, jewel-like centers of light all around the
"head" at the "forehead" level, and from it and the centers

---

3. See *The Kingdom of the Gods*, Plate 16, facing p. 225.
4. *Devi* is the feminine form of *Deva*.

flows up a slightly widening stream of diadem-like groups of forces.

I receive the impression of the presence of a considerable amount of purple in the aura of this great Devi and can add that, unlike the relatively immovable stability of the Deva, the Devi is free to move very high into the air. The function of this lofty being is hidden from me, save that "she" appears to be contributing almost star-like centers of power which "she" causes to blend with the inner aura of the Deva, thereby preserving a certain balance of interior energy by replacing the "quantities" of outpoured force.

From this Devi I receive the thought: "I preserve the balance of power within the central and more individual aspect of the Deva. As I do so, an interplay of positive and negative types of energy occurs between us, I myself hovering motionless while this is occurring. Thus, I both receive and contribute, although my function is largely, but not entirely, to help to preserve the central, individual 'form.' He is still; I am moving. He ever outpours; I continually pour in, thereby maintaining the equipoise or balance of various energies involved in the procedures for which we are both responsible in this area of the planet." The devic activity on the globe, deep within it and high above it, thus appears to be preserved in equipoise.

6

A Lofty Landscape Deva

Mt. Manaia Range, McLeod's Bay, Whangarei Heads

Presiding over the total range of mountains at Whangarei Heads—of which Mt. Manaia is at the southern end and a smaller mountain at the northern end—is a very lofty landscape Devaraja stationed above the center of the peaks, hovering normally at about half the height again of the summit of Mt. Manaia itself. [5] The central figure is almost immeasurably tall, at least the height of the mountain on the left, which would be some five hundred feet or more.

The lower portion of the aura, from the "shoulder" position outwards, embraces the whole range, over which the Deva appears to be in charge with regard to the devic stimulation of evolution in that area. The aura is thus very wide indeed. In color it is largely leaf-green and is in constant wave-like motion, each wave and large ripple shining with iridescent hues, including a sky blue and a very brilliant dark red. Power is simply pouring down upon us here in McLeod's Bay and even far beyond the harbor limits.

The upper aura of this truly tremendous being is violet down the center where "throat," "heart," and "solar plexus" would be, and is shining on either side with a color which I find difficult to describe. Fawn, glowing from within, would be the nearest, and beyond that more of the green and a touch of the violet of the aura which reaches to its outer edges. High above this, stretching from the "shoulder" position upwards, is the "head," which it is almost impossible to describe. An uprush of violet, green, and the brilliant fawn color, is streaming from the "shoulders" in a broad, widening band reaching outwards for at least a further two hundred feet. Above this, in turn, are spark-like, flashing centers of force, chiefly of the same colors. The "face" of the great Devaraja is just discernible, with an almost pointed "chin" and a marvelous halo of violet, fawn, and other colors shining all around and above it—indescribably magnificent. The sparks themselves give the impression of a jeweled crown high above the "head," producing the effect of majesty beyond description.

A brilliant center opens out in our direction from within the upper "head," the Devaraja being a very great height above us. Around its "shoulders," and still higher over the "head," numbers of sylphs are flying about within the aura, which reaches from Mt. Manaia to the other end of the range or ridge and gives the impression that immense, stimulating powers and forces are passing through the Devaraja downwards into the verdure and earth beneath. The Devaraja is thus quickening the evolution of the life within the area, and in addition from a position within, just below where the "heart" would be, a further concentration of the stimulating power descends from a higher plane—Atma, I presume—and, blending with the downpouring forces of the aura, thereby greatly increases their potency as a stimulant to evolutionary growth.

The two "eyes" are in their turn centers of radiation, producing in me a tremendous exaltation of consciousness as the great Devaraja bestows benediction upon our work. The

Painting by Marvin Richard Gratiot

5 *The Devaraja of Mt. Manaia Range, McLeod's Bay, Whangarei Heads*

whole area is alive with lesser Devas and sylphs, all in an intensely active state.

A Mountain God

On a later visit to Mt. Manaia, I observed at least five hundred feet above the summit rock the "denser" portion of the "form" of a Deva of magnificent appearance, with a central suggestion of a figure at least twenty feet tall. Above the "head" is an uprush of blue and violet light from the "shoulders" and the "crown," while at the outer edges streams of roseate apricot color reach up at least half as high as the height of the Deva itself. From the "shoulders" down to the "arms" and slightly sloping downwards into the mountain and surrounding air are surges of power—green, violet, and blue nearer the "body," shot through with shafts of white Atmic fire which follow the same path. On all sides and reaching here approximately one mile away is a powerfully stimulating inner potency of the life-force of the rock, the verdure, and the air, causing a tingling sensation as it flows through me into the earth beneath. Violet-illumined, flashing energies are thus radiating from all around the Deva into everything beneath. This outward and downward sloping force extends perhaps one hundred yards beyond the water's edge into the water of Whangarei Harbor. The lower and more outward areas of these currents contain much bright leaf-green, all such energies being self-radiant as if lighted from within.

The "heart" center is violet and white flecked with pale green, each color arranged in circles and pouring out from the Deva. This stream of energy also reaches us at the lower and higher mental levels of form-conceiving and formless thought, the "form" aspect of the Devaraja and its functions all appear to be most active at the lower mental level, so far

36

Painting by Gaile V. Campbell

6 *Archangels of the Sun*

Painting by Gaile V. Campbell

7 Solar Fire Lords

as the surface of the earth is concerned. The astro-etheric planes are powerfully affected, as if minute atom-like centers of white fire were continuously pouring out through the whole aura, being especially noticeable on these particular planes.

The life-force within the substances responds in a curious way, as if small "cylinders" were pointed upwards to receive and respond to the downpoured force. This makes the etheric double of the whole area tremendously alive—far more so than normally found—so that a kind of projected stimulus plays into the atoms and molecules wherein the life-principle is incarnated, the evolutionary procedure being quickened thereby.

The right-hand peak of Mt. Manaia is like a lighthouse from which this phenomenon is issuing at high intensity. High above this aspect of the Devaraja, in the uppermost regions of the aura, a coronet effect is produced by concentrated up-rushing forces. These arise from the region of the crown of the "head," within which there shine numerous jewel-like, living and flashing centers of light—purple, mauve, violet, ruby, and gold—while at the upper part of this coronet an uprush of purely white forces is rising. In addition, an effect of a brilliantly radiant white garment or surplice composed of streaming energies surrounds the outer edges of the main aura. It is vividly alive and vibrating, and power is passing through it both from without and from within, bestowing an extraordinary beauty and grace to the whole appearance of this most wonderful Devaraja.

The "eyes" are proportionately large, probably six or even more inches in diameter, and are obviously vehicles or instruments for observation by the innermost Self of the Devaraja of all that is occurring, including the attempted descriptions.

The "third eye" or chakram at the "forehead" similarly radiates a powerful stream or current of white and yellow power for several feet out into the air—or, rather, the formless, higher mental plane. This performs the twofold function of perception and the projection of awareness-stimulating energy.

While physically the mountain occupies a limited locality and the geographical range of the downward-driven, quickening forces is limited, no such isolations and insulations exist at the higher levels. The Deva is thus to a very large extent spatially unrestricted, particularly so far as awareness itself is concerned and, if I may presume to say so, also concerning the passage of time.

Although intensely and powerfully engaged in assigned responsibility as "Devaraja evolution-quickener" of this region, this being is also in collaboration with the Mahadevaraja of the planet as a whole.

In addition, I perceive that a vast coordinated devic activity at all levels is continuously maintained under a hierarchy of Devas, from newly individualized sylphs up to the great Devic Lord of the planet itself. If I may dare to say so, I think that this, in its turn, is part of the activity of the Lords of the planets of the solar system itself. [6, 7]

The Mahadevic consciousness is thus occupied with interior and superior levels and beings, and with the directive thought by which all outer functions are controlled.

7

Deva of the Harbor

Bream Head Mount, Whangarei

This Deva is serving not only the evolving earth and water life, but is also responsible for shipping and passengers and for their safe entry into Whangarei Harbor. [8] Unlike the other Devas already studied, this being is directing its awareness out to sea and across the entrance to the harbor.

As if communicating, the Deva explains: "Unlike my brothers, I am equally concerned with the evolving life-spirit in the air above and all around me, though more especially across the harbor entrance to the land beyond. Also, I am assisting the evolution of the life in the mineral and plant kingdoms within this mount and over a wide range below." I now see a "bridge," very long indeed, of devic "quickening" energy. As the clairvoyant investigation continues, I note the same downward, out-spreading radiation of power from the Deva where the "shoulders" would be, into the world beneath some four hundred feet above the topmost rock, ministering in the way described above.

The entire form of the Deva to "shoulders" and "neck" is also surrounded by an aura of energy outflowing laterally into the air, all around for a distance of some one hundred yards or more. The color is purple shot through with white fire, changing to green halfway up, and to yellow where the throat and heart would be. Up from the "shoulders," a widening stream of power flows high above the Deva's "head." Its shadings include rose, apricot, and luminous fawn, with the same purple color in the area some fifteen or twenty feet around the "head." Within and blended with these, in an unpatterned manner, there is much grey-blue, unlike any other Deva's aura I have ever seen. This upward-radiating, outspreading auric force does not wholly follow a straight line. I am amazed to see that the outer layers open out as they rise in a curve as does a flower, while the uprising force from the "body" and "head" maintains the widening, straight, streaming shape on the whole.

The Kundalini force also, I now see, is flowing—almost rushing—up from far below the ground, perhaps the center of the earth, in a flaming red and gold stream, following what in man would be the region of the spinal column but wider, occupying most of the back of the Deva form. The threefold Kundalini pattern is visible within the stream.

This current leaps across the space between the surface of the earth and the lower aura or form of the Deva, and thence rises vertically and passes out at the top of the head in a fiery, upward-soaring flame. It is one part of the power used by the Deva for its terrestrial ministrations. I presume that in essence this Deva is associated with the solar and planetary Kundalini, and is functioning in some deeply occult and mystical collaboration concerning the role within nature of Kundalini Shakti. This locality where I am at present studying extends for two or three miles around Bream Head, and is an area of considerable Kundalini activity—a kind of Kundalini volcano arising from the center of the earth where the great *Fire* is stored.

Painting by Marvin Richard Gratiot

8 The Deva of Bream Head Mount, Whangarei

I receive a hailing or greeting from the wonderful being, who addresses me as follows, as if from one brother to another: "I perceive the same Fire established and active within yourself. Greetings, Kundalini brother. Devas are of many orders, and one of these may be referred to as *Kundalini Devas*, of which I am privileged to be one, having been thus 'conceived' by the great Lord of all that exists."

8

Devic Life of the Mountains

Mt. Ngauruhoe and Nearby Mountains, North Island

The reigning Devaraja appears several hundred feet above the mountain top and draws my attention to the "ladder" or "steps" of intercommunion from and between the Devaraja within the crater—the very active Hephaestus-like being— the mountain Deva itself, and also a still greater Mahadeva presiding over the whole area of Tongariro. This includes Mt. Ruapehu and other mountains extending for some thirty miles in all directions from the Chateau Tongariro. This great one is, in its turn, at one with the major landscape Mahadeva of the earth as a whole—an angelic presence of immeasurable stature.

Within the lower portion of the aura of this latter planetary Devaraja [9], there shines a blend of grass-green and deep sky-blue. From where the spine would be there rises out of the center of the earth the planetary Kundalini-Shakti, a mighty power indeed. Closely examined, this triple force is seen to flow upward, Kundalini-like, with a very wide cylindrical uprush of "fire" enclosing the threefold current. This ascends far above the high aura and upper radiations into areas beyond my range of vision towards, I venture to presume, the Logos of our planetary scheme. This "ladder" extends upwards into the Solar Logos itself, whom I can only faintly and very reverently conceive of as a vast, sky-filling, intensely glowing radiance of golden power and light.

I am only able to describe the Mahadeva for whom Mt. Ngauruhoe is, as it were, a physical focal point or "throne" [10] as a center of power whose responsibilities extend beyond New Zealand, and so beyond my capacity to observe. Outwards from the "shoulders" I gradually note forces sweeping out and raying forth, some slantingly, from the upper part of the "body," while the heart chakram is a most wonderful sun-like, whirling center of outrushing, brilliantly colored power—purple, green, roseate pink, red, and golden, with many other hues produced by the blendings of these shades.

I can only bow in reverent homage before this great one, in gratitude for the privilege of being granted awareness of its presence while visiting the volcanic mountain above which the Devaraja would seem to be stationed, or rather enthroned.

The mountain's mass itself is clearly being subjected to an inertia-reducing, responsiveness-increasing condition, a quickening of the evolution of both the life and the sub-stances associated therewith. Hosts of salamanders or nature spirits of Fire of varying degrees of development and stature are seen to be collaborating in this planetary "blacksmith's" work.[1] Thus the whole interior of the volcano—especially where I am observing it at the level of the lower slopes and earth surface—is being intensely "worked upon" by sala-manders and the volcanic Deva in charge of them, in order to participate in the great planetary and systemic urge or

---

1. See *Kingdom of the Gods,* p. 211.

Painting by Frank A. Eden

9 *Landscape Mahadeva of the Earth as a Whole*

Painting by Frank A. Eden

10 Devaraja within Mt. Ngauruhoe, North Island

increasing drive to bring about the evolution-quickening procedure. I have come to believe this quickening fulfills the whole purpose of the existence of the universe, all its beings, greater and lesser, and all its component parts.

I presume that volcanoes differ from all other mountains in that the element of Fire from deeper down within the planet is in them actively employed by devic ministrants for the carrying out of this wholly impersonal, universally operative urge towards evolutionary unfoldment. The consciousness of members of the devic hierarchy, from nature sprite to archangel, I now perceive consists of laughter-filled joy. This could be a yogic ideal for human attainment. Admittedly this can be very difficult, if not impossible, especially for those who are enduring karmic sadness, whether physical from ill-health or psychological from sufferings of the heart and the mind.

These Fire Devas appear to be "digging" into and loosening the structure of the etheric and physical "lining" of the crater, and even beyond it for several yards into the interior.[11] The life-principle in the atoms and molecules of the substance glows increasingly as this occult, devic ministration continues. The process takes place deep within the crater even below the base of the mountain where—using the Blacksmith simile—the great planetary forge is burning, this being a continuance of the same activities deeper into the earth.

On further observing the great Devaraja of Mt. Ngauruhoe [10], I find on the left side where the "hip" would be the principal colors are grass-green near the "waist" and then a brilliant sky blue for the whole of the "hip," extending to below the "knee" area. This blue spreads out for at least one hundred yards on the left side of the Deva in all directions, especially from the "shoulders" to up above the "head"

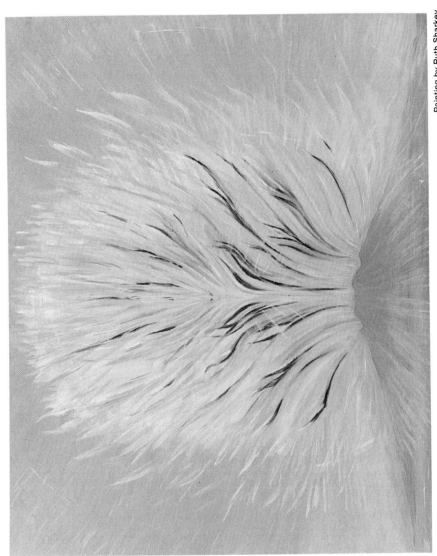

11 *Rangitoto Island Deva, Auckland*

from where it extends at least two hundred feet and blends with a brilliant white radiation from the whole aura.

The left side of the aura below the blue is radiant with a rosy-red glow, which expands skirt-like right round the lower portion of the aura and reaches out for a least one hundred yards. This white radiance also descends below the "feet" deep down towards and into the crater. The upper right side of the devic aura is also sky blue at the regions of the "shoulders" and "neck," with the radiant rose below that area.

The "throat" chakram is very bright, the colors being chiefly white and gold, while through the crown an uprush of fiery power is shooting along the "spinal" area, Kundalini-like, and far up above the "head," reaching into heights beyond. In the center of the "head," radiant at the place where the eyes would be, is an outraying white and sky blue force, with other colors blended within the enormous funnel of the brow chakram. Deep within, I now gradually learn, is a profound stillness of consciousness, far beyond the limitations of personality and concrete thought. At this level the Devaraja is wonderfully crowned with a golden uprushing radiance, shot through and at places glowing with the same rosy-red coloring—a godlike crown indeed!

Although the higher consciousness would seem to exist in poised stillness, the more formal mind is aware throughout this region and, I venture to suggest, reaches out as far as Rangitoto (Auckland Harbor) and Bream Head Mountain (Whangarei Harbor Heads) and the Kundalini fire and volcanic fires within both of them. The system of correspondences is actively at work, and the range of communication is virtually planetary. Indeed, the words come to mind: "A Devaraja of the embodied and incarnated Kundalini Shakti of the planet, of which order many others exist and function in New Zealand."

9

Devas of the Plant Kingdom

Cornwall Park, Auckland

This great being is "stationed" above the summit of One Tree Hill Mountain within Cornwall Park, Epsom, Auckland. [12] The outstanding auric color is a brilliant gold radiating from the region of the "head" and extending upwards for at least one hundred feet. This portion of the devic aura can be described as funnel-shaped, with the lower opening within the region of the "head." Thereafter, it widens, glowing, as it rises at least forty feet to the upper portion of the inner aura.

Streaming outwards from the position of the "body" is a bright leaf or grass green auric force. Within that color is observable the intensely glowing chakras arising from the position of the "head," "throat," "heart," and where the base of the spine would be in a human being. These chakras are spinning rapidly and appear to be in size somewhat as follows:

Crown of "head"—six feet and golden.
"Brow"—three feet and a darker yellow, with flashes of sky-blue and white.
"Throat"—almost entirely blue, with a golden "heart," and reaching out for some two feet.

Painting by Angela Meeson

12 Deva of Cornwall Park, Auckland

13 New Zealand Tree Fern Deva

"Heart"—gold, bright green, and blue with white rays flashing through. Almost immeasurable.

Base of "spine"—directly in contact with the center of the earth, from which Kundalini is flowing up and out the top of the "head," with the fiery red color of the power glowing at its center and rising upwards high into the sky, flame-like, very potent, with continual flashes of brilliant white.

The whole of these aspects of the aura shine forth at the level of intelligence or higher and lower manas. Again I observe the flashes and streams of fiery white extending outwards even beyond the edge of the far-reaching aura, which is actually immeasurable from my present location but at least twenty yards from the "form," with the brightest hues extending far beyond.

In addition, I perceive what I can only describe as devic auric powers which reach beyond the form and are capable of being made to stretch out, touch, and stimulate the life-principle throughout the whole park. This phenomenon is very notable from the place where we are seated and is observed to be active on all sides of the hill, including the obelisk on the summit.

Hosts of lesser Devas and nature spirits are within the range of this aura. All are hyperactive, the nature spirits being in continual movement, which seems to increase when the devic centers of power are concentrated in their areas.

This great Deva is a head of a very large group of plant kingdom Devas and nature spirits, especially including those associated with trees, every one of which within this particular area is seen to be within the influence of the Mahadeva itself. [13] All the members of the devic hierarchy, from nature spirits upwards, are under the care of the same great being. While nature spirits and the Devas of the smaller trees are quite unaware of this ministration, all Devas of the astral and lower mental planes are consciously—even if somewhat automatically—aware and responsive.

The primary interest and activity of the Cornwall Park Deva is, of course, within the area of the actual park over which it presides, and especially concerns the major responsibilities of such an office, but the area of radius of its influence is not limited either to the region of One Tree Hill itself or even of Cornwall Park. So wonderfully brilliant is the whole form and aura of the Deva that it stimulates a continual evolution-quickening, development-hastening, and sensitivity-increasing process for the One Life unfolding within the mineral content of the earth and for the plant kingdom, from the simplest grass and weeds to the trees, both evergreen and deciduous. Even the life locked up in the obelisk at the summit receives this continuous stimulation.

I receive the impression of a kind of empire over which the presiding Deva has charge. As I watch this, I perceive a certain mental interchange also occurring, as if the great Deva were instructing me concerning the wholly mysterious functions which members of that order are carrying out. These, I now see, include the "growth according to design" principle by which all plant life, indeed all life, is ruled.

A Communication from the Great Cornwall Park Deva

The function of those Devas named landscape Devas is to quicken the evolution of all life in the landscape—submineral, mineral, and plant from miniature plants to the most gigantic of all trees such as redwoods. Within all of these there resides and evolves the One Divine Life. Every atom, every molecule of combined atoms, and every cell—all of these are in themselves the one embodiment of the one living, evolving element in the sense that they consist of created, life-filled matter.

Just as for the human kingdom wherein self-consciousness has been attained in varying degrees, so also every member of every subhuman kingdom is undergoing the dual process of a natural unfoldment and a stimulated development. In the human kingdom, and in equally evolved members of the angelic hosts, this is carried out by both superhuman beings or adepts and members of the angelic hierarchy. On behalf of the life which is indwelling in every atom of all the subhuman kingdoms, a quickening force or power is being perpetually brought to play.

In what may perhaps be named the Aerial kingdom— meaning not birds but elementals of nature which are members of the Air and Fire kingdoms and are evolving through them—this universal procedure is carried out by two classes of beings, unconsciously and instinctually by those who have not attained separated selfhood (fairies, for example), and consciously by those who have already done so.

Thus regarded, the universe is purely and simply a mighty school and evolution-speeding establishment, and evidence of advancement in this process consists of not only knowledge of its existence but also—and far more importantly—of the provision of opportunities for participation in The Great Work.

If this view is accepted, then the one standard whereby an individual's stage of development can be assessed would be the degree of participation, with increasing effectiveness, intelligence and power, in the process of aiding the innermost function of all nature. This is nothing less than perpetual unfoldment or, to use a simpler word, growth. This impulse to grow is imparted to the inherent life-principle which "lives" in everything that exists. As age upon age passes, this process not only continues, but increases in energized activity.

Angelic Healing

In addition to these and still other activities, which include those of higher mental and supramental orders of Devas, the ministration of the Cornwall Park Deva is seen to include help rendered on behalf of the unfortunate people at the Green Lane Hospital admitted as patients and those visiting. [14] I also observe that the intellects of physicians who are sufficiently responsive sometimes receive guidance in the form of tendencies to respond to instinctual ideas—especially when a mystery exists concerning a patient's condition. This service also applies on occasion to matrons and nurses who, without being aware of the fact, receive flashes of intuition which often, unconsciously to themselves, indicate special methods of treatment and general care.

A totally different order of Devas is, however, involved in operations, recoveries, and the healing of wounds. These have little if any relationship with archangels of nature. Their contribution consists of the direction into wounds, organs, brains, and nerves, of unifying, even building, superphysical energies, chiefly higher and lower mental and astral, the etheric effects following naturally. I notice a lofty healing Deva associated with a particular ward, who is carrying out these functions more directly and personally, especially as karmic law permits; for this law, of course, plays a very significant, indeed decisive, part in healing processes and their effects.

14 *Cornwall Park Deva Aiding in Adjacent Hospital*

A sublimely beautiful archangel, in collaboration with the Cornwall Park Deva, is supervising all devic and even nature spirit functions at the hospital, assistance being given wherever permissible and advisable. This aid, in part, takes the form of streams of both thought—cell-building thought, for example—and currents of spiritual and higher mental forces welling up, as it were, within the bodies of sufferers, and also descending upon them, sometimes in quite small streams of intensely concentrated power.

Every single patient, every sufferer, receives such ministrations, the forms of which are exceedingly numerous. Those involved in accidents and other sudden occurrences are immediately visited, and every possible and karmically allowable devic and nature spirit assistance is made available. A close intercommunication and collaboration continually occurs between the two presiding Devas—the Cornwall Park Deva and the Green Lane Hospital Deva. Above, and in unity with both of them, presides a still greater being, which appears to be a representative of the Deva either of the North Island or of New Zealand as a whole—the former, I am inclined to think.

In addition, mysterious as it may seem, an archangel associated with the Tasman Sea and certain other very lofty supramental Devas participate in the evolution and experiences of human life in New Zealand, while doubtless this applies to the oceans of the eastern coasts as well; for at those levels divisions of kingdoms and countries have little significance, all life being known as *inseparably One.*

10

The Golden Deva

Mt. Tongariro, North Island

I am aware of the presence nearby of a very remarkable golden Deva which hovers near a fellow student and myself. [15] At the formless levels it pours into us a force resembling liquid sunlight and also focuses a special ray upon the centers of solar power in the middle of our physical and superphysical heads, causing them to glow as if on fire. The Deva's form appears as molten gold, and rays of life-force and light flow out beside and behind it. The whole of the Deva's aura is formed of pointed beams or tongues of outflowing streams of extremely fine texture of the golden, glowing One Life. These rays shine out over the "head" and right down to the "feet," and are most closely focused behind the positions of the "heart" and the "solar plexus," where the color deepens to a more orange-hued gold. The "hair," radiations of life-force from the "head," consists of smaller tongues of golden light. The "eyes" below the broad and noble "brow" in their turn appear as pools of solar light and life, with a will-center behind them of extraordinary intensity and power.

The Deva seems unaware of and unresponsive to the four vehicles of the personality which are below its level of consciousness, its whole attention being focused on the buddhic vehicle and plane, of which it appears to be an archangel denizen. This great being now indicates that at such level the sole purpose for the existence of the angelic hierarchy, and of all human beings, seems to be to obtain fuller, freer, and less personally limited expressions of the One Life. The Deva implied that this is more than channelship; for the making and widening of funnels and chakras is supplemented by fuller realization by the Ego of identity with the One Life, so that each individual may become a complete manifestation or manifestor of that Life. This attainment depends upon the condition of the Buddhic sheath, larval in the mass of humanity, chrysalis-like in a small number, and freed and winged in the initiates of the globe. The last-named stage permits the development and expansion of the Buddhic vehicle and consciousness, this being the work and ideal of an initiate of the great white Brotherhood of adepts.

The human consciousness, and as far as possible the personality, must become increasingly aware of the One Life of the Solar Logos itself, and must know by experience that the Buddhic vehicle and the Buddhic Self are manifestations of that Life, being identical therewith. The One Life appears to be a shoreless, golden, glowing ocean, completely impersonal and universal. It is, however, the Buddhic vehicle of the Solar Logos or Lord of our solar system and only seems boundless because the human being cannot perceive its limits, if such exist. Apparently the Buddhic vestures of all Dhyanis or highest spiritual beings must merge into, and be part of, the vestures of a larger Lord, culminating in that of the cosmic Logos, the One Lord of All. The sole purpose of the so-called Buddhic exercises of an initiate is to bring about both an increase of the universal, Buddhic presence and life in the initiate's Buddhic body, and an increasing and

62

Painting by Frank A. Eden

15 *A Golden Deva, Tongariro, North Island*

deepening realization of the Buddhic aspect of the Solar Logos and of unity therewith. The whole of the Great White Brotherhood has its Buddhic expression and vesture, which is merged in the Buddhic vestures of the Lord of the World, the Silent Watcher, and their seniors, so that in very truth *all are one and one is all.*

At this level the sense of separation has vanished and the aura does not look as if it has an edge. All beings appear to be merged in the "shining sea,"[1] as are raindrops after falling into a lake or bubbles rising through liquid and disappearing into the air. Yet, strangely enough, there remains an I-consciousness which nevertheless does not show evidence of having its own separate vehicle, but rather uses quite freely any area of the "shining sea" completely without the sense of possessing that area, or even of living within an auric envelope. The effect of the Deva's ministrations upon the aura is to add a golden glow and cause rays to appear round and above the "head," like those round the head of the Grecian Helios.

Such terms and concepts as universe, Logos, and One Self almost lose their significance at this level where divisions are not discernible. The accent is upon oneness, singleness, wholeness, the totality with which awareness is so absorbed that individuality of any kind is relegated to the unreal and the non-essential.

The effect upon waking consciousness of this realization of Oneness is of complete harmonization, integration, and of having been smoothed, as it were, from within outwards. Problems, both intellectual and of the karma and conduct of

1. See Sir Edwin Arnold, *The Light of Asia* (Adyar: Theosophical Publishing House, 1982).

life and limitations of development, do continue to exist for such a person, but without stress. Furthermore, the sense of time-pressure is reduced to a minimum, as also to some extent is that of the restriction of distance, somewhat as when a journey by land and sea occupying days is completed by air in a few hours and with remarkable ease. The physical body seems to have lost its weight, as if poised buoyantly in air.

The planet Earth is itself charged with currents of golden, liquid life-force flowing swiftly over and under the surface, aerating the globe as it were, or rather infiltrating it with Buddhic life. The lines of force—the word is inappropriate because at these levels there is no stress—form an intricate network which produces the impression of intensely active, conscious life, busily but rhythmically and continuously at work, somewhat like a colony of ants inside its ant-hill. The air, too, is similarly filled, and so are all structures and growing things. There is, for example, a suggestion of an individual network within plants, trees, animals, and human bodies, as if each had its own web of Life. The life itself, however, is the same in all, but conforms somewhat to the bodily shape. The form of every human being is thrilling with this life, which is intensely, busily, and consciously active within the body, almost like bees in a hive. It constantly provides minute stimuli, vital "food," and the element of coordinated, purposeful constructiveness to every cell and organ. From this superphysical point of view this element becomes invisible and only the network of form remains, with its innumerable strands and loops of extremely fine mesh. Small explosions appear to be occurring all the time within the web and also in the open spaces between the strands, as the life-force arrives and is continuously liberated into the body. In ill health there is doubtless some local disruption of this coordinated structure and activity, and healing can be brought about by its restoration.

11

An Archangel of Sea Water

Eastern Beach, near Auckland

In undertaking this research, I have been granted the privilege of experiencing at least *dual* vision. One part of this consisted in awareness of the existence of a great Devarani of somewhat feminine character, concerned with the North Island of New Zealand as a whole, particularly in its "Water Devi" characteristic [16]. The second aspect of the vision included the Devarani of the element of Water for at least this region of the Pacific Ocean, and also for all levels associated with New Zealand itself, especially the North Island and its lakes. [17].

My consciousness was then linked with Lake Taupo, where another great feminine-like Devarani was present, hovering partly above and partly below the surface of the water. I realized that there exists a supremely great "feminine" Devarani for the North Island, and also a manifestation of the principle of which that being is a representative and an expression.

Although at this lofty level a certain form-like being did reveal itself most graciously, the whole phenomenon was really manifest largely, if not only, at the level of higher manas. I then saw that it would be necessary to study this

Painting by Frank A. Eden

16 *An Archangel of the North Island, seen at Mt. Tongariro*

experience at two almost separate levels: the purely formless or the principle of Water Devaranis of a country or very large district; the apparently lesser evolved manifestations of that principle seen on occasions at specific places and in particular forms, with auras and chakras as already described elsewhere.

As I experimentally investigated, I observed that the Element of Water, whether fresh or salt, tends to be less differentiated in general appearance than the Elements of Earth or Fire, particularly Earth. Air, in its turn, is the most formless to the five human senses. If, however, the Element of Ether is included, then this also appears to be formless. On the other hand, nature spirits associated with the Element of Earth—gnomes, for example—when fully observed seem to possess human-like bodies. Nature spirits of Water may be said to manifest almost formlessly except for stream-like and wave-like shapes.

Continuing my research, I now see the great archangel "queen" as a being of immense power whose lower streams of energy resemble curved shell forms. [17] I am suddenly and very deeply impressed by the region occupied by the "heart" chakram which, when viewed as now from in front, is spinning counterclockwise. The "heart" is, however, a center of outflung forces arising from deeper levels, and these combine with the circular movements of the whirling chakram to produce a very wonderful and beautiful group of effects. The central color is deep rose, this shade also being present at the edges of other parts of the chakram. Blended within the whole are wonderful radiations of sea green and golden yellow which also shoot forth and spiral outwards from the very center of the chakram, while within is a lovely sky blue. The "throat" chakram is also visible, colored somewhat as is

17 An Archangel of Sea Water, Eastern Beach near Auckland

the blue lotus chakram of human beings,[1] and this shines forth far beyond where the "shoulders" would be. These, together with the "spinal" and "head" currents, sweep up, spreading outwards high into the air as they do so.

A gloriously beautiful human-like "face" with wonderful "eyes" occupies the normal position. Above the enlarged "forehead" there streams outwards from the whole aura in lateral, intertwining and vertical directions a magnificent, very radiant summit or "crown," reaching far upwards above the "head."

The center and range of consciousness of this being, as far as its "individuality" is concerned, may be described as Atmic, Buddhic, and higher Manasic, even though the Devarani is also capable of awareness at the levels of form. Thus, I observe, the whole of sea and fresh water life and living inhabitants are under the evolutionary guidance and evolution-quickening care and influence of a very great order of Water Mahadevaranis.

The superphysical levels of the Elements of Water, both salt and fresh, in the neighborhood of such a being as I am attempting to describe, continually receive unbroken streams or currents of power, perhaps superphysically electrified. In addition, as I now observe, all plants, seaweeds, and other appropriate structures, are also recipients of the same evolu- tion-quickening energy. Thus, strange as it may seem at first, the great Mahadevis of Water are both agents for and trans- mitters of immensely powerful forces. These affect not only the indwelling life of the water, but also the age-long evolu- tionary developments of all matter and all forms associated with the Element of Water. This applies to all parts of nature which are living, growing, and unfolding therein.

---

1. See C. W. Leadbeater, *The Chakras.*

As I attempt to merge my consciousness with these processes I also perceive the presence of Devas ranging from undine or Water Mahadevis to nature spirits at the etheric levels, similarly at work. Throughout all this order of beings flow the evolution-producing spiritual, mental, and submental powers which originate from the One Divine Source or, to use a philosophical and occult term, The One Alone.

Such, although but imperfectly and incompletely referred to, is the function of the wondrous devic "Queen" whom I have been privileged to study during visits to the area of these researches. This function also applies to the hierarchy of devic intelligences of a solar system, planet, order of living beings and creatures, and growing plants and minerals.

How difficult it would be for an artist to present an accurate illustration in which the surface of the ocean is portrayed halfway down the picture. Above this would be the undine Mahadevi as already described, while below—within the water, as it were—the lower portion of the aura of the Mahadevi would be seen to consist, not of relatively straight outrushings of colored auric energy, but in some way of wave-like radiations. This occurs while the central form still maintains dignity and even grandeur.

The whole underwater area, seen clairvoyantly, is delicately colored pale blue and green, the lower portion of the aura of the Mahadevi being more clearly indicated with rather long and wave-like curves. The upper, outflowing forces are elongated and graceful, while the lower ones suggest undulating downflowings which continue as far as the interior of the lower aura but do not actually give the impression of limbs. These downward flowing forces appear to be more heavily colored than the upper portion of the aura, being dark blue and green, almost approaching indigo and heavy leaf-green.

71

This truly great Mahadevirani is crowned with white and gold energy uprushing above the "head," with tinges of fiery red faintly showing, and the position of the "eyes" indicated by similar radiations. The chakram at the top of the "head" is seen to be more brilliant than the "crown" itself. As is the case with all Devas and Devis, the usual somewhat wing-like, upward and outward curving auric streams are clearly visible, while beyond the aura, in fainter colors, radiations continue far above into the air.

II

*Esoteric Effects
of Music*

The Purpose of the Clairvoyant Research

Mr. Hodson's research into the effects of music was concentrated along the following lines:

1. The effects on the surrounding astro-mental material.
2. The effects on the performers.
3. Responses from the Deva kingdom.
4. The effects on the listeners.

To achieve these ends Mr. Hodson requested Mr. Murray Stentiford to suggest lines of research for each particular piece of music.

The pieces were of short duration and, in the main, were chosen by the performers. Being short, each example could be repeated in part or in whole as Mr. Hodson required.

Portions of two recorded works were also played to Mr. Hodson for comparison with the effects of the live performances.

HUGH DIXON

12

The Power of Music

Beautiful music could save and ugly, debased music degrade mankind, so great is the power of sound itself. Music generates strong influences which penetrate the auras of all within range, stirring up corresponding responses and, in some cases, the emotions and minds of the hearers. This is the way that singing and all music influence listeners. Very strong currents working through the source of the sound enter their auras and "set up" the corresponding mental, emotional, and physical responses. This occurs in addition to such general effects as the import of the song, the kind of music, and its effects on people and on nature itself.

Song-streams and the general radiation has beneficial, neutral, or harmful effects upon listeners. Singing or instrumental music works upon their auras, producing longing, love of nature, or degrading desires, stimulating corresponding chakras and organs of the body. Harmonious, joyful music produces happiness and upliftment affecting the upper part of the aura—heart, throat, head and reaching the Ego or immortal Self within, if responsive. Degrading, coarse music is very harmful, especially to the lower half of the aura and body.

My studies reveal that music is a potent power in the hands of musicians. It can exalt and illumine or degrade, with half-way stages in between, all according to the type of music, the thought, influence, and character of the performer and, of course, the listener.

This is surely natural since the universe and all that it contains is generated or created by the emission of cosmic and universal creative sounds, the great choruses of the Ghandarvas, music Devas, taking up the themes and with them filling and shaping the space to be formed into universes. Furthermore, one may assume that, while performing, every true musician is brought into relationship with the Ghandarvas or archangels of creative sound and can become a channel for their uplifting influences. Musicians are thus presumed to be effective agents for creative energy which, particularly if it is of a more spiritual nature, is poured forth into the world and into people's lives. It must be remembered, however, that as in the creation of universes the archangels and angels of song thus participate, but only in the purest, highest, and most elevating form of music.

Other Devas are evidently also involved with music, particularly those connected with what I may refer to as the mathematics of creation, for as Plato said, "God geometrizes." There are orders of angels whose consciousness is largely at the higher and lower mental levels only. They are concerned with the intricate geometrical processes associated with the physical manifestation of the divine Idea expressed as sound. Composers and performers are in contact with these also, and it may be that great Egos have been and will be inspired, not only from their own Egos or immortal Selves, but with the aid of the angelic hosts.

When such communications are received by the mind, the knowledge awakens *within*, rather than impinging from without. The procedure is not actually clairaudience, since no occult sound is every heard. During the reception, the recipient experiences a "mento-verbal" teaching from without. Nevertheless, the true spirituo-mystic communication is actually "awakened" within the recipient's mind. This is somewhat like a teacher saying to a student: "Do you see that lighthouse over there?" and the student replying: "Yes, I do see both the lighthouse itself and at the same time the light shining from within it."

My own limited faculty of clairvoyance has confirmed for me that physical sounds are creative and produce movement, color, and forms in astral and mental substances. The main purposes of the investigations recorded in this section were to discover the different effects produced by the performance of music upon the adjacent matter of the superphysical worlds, upon the musicians and the audience, and to study the responses of Devas. For a discussion of the procedure and some of the difficulties of clairvoyant investigation of music forms, see "A Clairvoyant Study of Music," in my book *Music Forms*,[1] a book which concentrates only on the superphysical forms.

The results of my attempted clairvoyant research were carefully described and recorded while each performance was proceeding, often with repetitions of the music in accordance with my request. Mr. Frank Eden then produced fine oil paintings from the descriptions. It is my hope that the paintings themselves will both give pleasure and evoke an interest in the subject matter which they illustrate.

---

1. *Music Forms* (Adyar: Theosophical Publishing House, 1979).

13

"Ave Maria"

Schubert

The poetry of this beautiful supplication to the Virgin Mary was written by Sir Walter Scott, being No. 6 of his "Lady of the Lake" songs. It was sung in German by Wendy Dixon, unaccompanied, on two separate occasions with a gap of three weeks between, followed by a cello rendition by Wendy.

The music sets up a continuous song-ribbon. That is, in addition to wide-ranging effects, all notes when sounded or sung produce a typical form in superphysical matter. These forms are colored by the way the sound is produced, and the size of the form is determined by the length of time in which a note is sounded or sung. In the playing or singing of an air or tune, these successive note forms are linked together and the whole sequence is interconnected. The variations in shape are much more observable when the notes are sung than when played on a musical instrument, hence my term "song-ribbon." For illustrations of song-ribbons, see paintings no. 20, 23, and 26.

The singer's aura becomes greatly enlarged, extending to the walls of the house and beyond. Her personality opens so that her aura is tuned to interchange with the Ego or Atma-Buddhi-Manas, the threefold, immortal, unfolding spiritual

Self. At this point the brilliance of the colors of her aura increases; blue from the eyes to the heart region brightens as she sings, and green and gold in two antler-like streams appear above the head. The major effects are still obvious after five minutes.

With the first line an uprush of energy streams from her shoulders high into the air. Along with this appears increasing activity of the heart and throat chakras, and increased blue, as already stated.

With the second line comes a waving outflow of the whole aura in green, gold, and blue, as the rise and fall of the notes becomes clairvoyantly visible and audible. The uprushing antler effect increases.

The third line affects the lower third of the aura. This is much slower in responding but does so as the verse continues, though never, so far, as intensely as the upper two-thirds. There are nature spirits all around the singer, on the floor and permeating her, the lower third of her aura being elevated instinctively by this condition.

Halfway through the first verse the crown chakram definitely opens, and forces along the spine flow increasingly upwards along the channel of the sushumna, a channel for Kundalini. This is safe for the singer and of assistance to the effects of her singing.

All the etheric emanations and the whole of the astral and mental bodies become unified by the singing, and by the end of the third verse increase in their actual dimensions from about two yards all round her to at least one-third more. Towards the end of the verse purple and dark green increase in the lower third of the aura.

When the song is repeated from the beginning, at the high

note a rush of yellow slightly edged with green shoots from the region of the lungs and voice up through shoulders. This remains until the end as part of the general auric change with which it is blended.

There is a noticeable extension of the health aura, part of the etheric double, from a normal one-and-a-half inches to about five inches, the whole glowing with extra light.[1] This continues after the close of the first verse. I assume that beneficial health effects have been produced, though the performer would seem to be in good health naturally.

The last verse, sung again with full feeling and recognition of the meaning, produces an uprush of twenty inches with a radial effect in the singer's aura, followed by another uprush.

The third singing of the second verse produces effects similar to those described regarding increase in size and differences within the auric mento-astral from about the solar plexus upwards. This again becomes illumined, enlightened, enlarged with streams of high thought force shooting up at the high notes. The lower part of the aura responds more to the appeal and even to the sadness of the words, drooping a little, taking the form from waist downwards of a very wide, full skirt to and below the ground, in green, purple, and some grey.

The performer reads aloud the words of Verse 3 in English. There is a great reduction of the effects described, largely due to the action of the mind of the reader, plus her memories and normal responses.

---

1. The health aura is an emanation of the physical body, and its condition is greatly affected by one's health. For a description and picture of the health aura, see C. W. Leadbeater, *Man Visible and Invisible*, (Wheaton, Il.: Theosophical Publishing House, 1975), Chapter XX.—Ed.

Then she sings the last verse again. The rear part of her aura is more responsive and extends with two distinctively wing-shaped outrushes of energy from the body position. This verse increases the general effect of the blending of the inner Ego with the astro-mental bodies and personality as a whole, thereby bringing the effects to their apparently highest beneficence.

The Words "Ave Maria"

When the words "Ave Maria" are sung, they produce a great increase in intensity and liveliness, and the effects extend to a greater distance, much to the health benefit of the singer, despite the fatigue from standing so long. The last two notes of "Maria" produce blue and yellow.

Again "Maria" is sung by itself. The song-ribbon effect is confirmed, each contributory part of the ribbon being responsive to note for color; strength of singing for size; length of holding the note for elongation; and the consonant for the end of the shape.

When the words are sung once again, in addition to the colors already mentioned a deep and very beautiful rose appears, nearly but not completely ruddy. The singer's brow chakram greatly increases, extending at least four inches in front of the skin over the brow.

Angelic Responses

One beautiful angel, chiefly blue but with the colors of the song also noticeable, hovers in the air about two yards behind and slightly to the left of the singer, with its head at a similar

81

distance above the singer's head. This angel is responding to the rhythm of the movement as if, though not actually, beating time, the whole aura waving with the rhythm of the music. A brilliant five-pointed star shines above the forehead of the Deva who is blessing the singer and, through her, the listeners. I presume this angel to be a representative member of the angelic order functional under that great angelic being Our Blessed Lady, and therefore a bearer of her blessing to and through the performer to the hearers.

The auras of the four of us present become tinged in front with Our Lady's blue. This color is far more brilliant than any painting could possibly display; it is intense, as if interiorly glowing. Our auras are now shining with this influence, including Murray Stentiford's, who is sitting to the rear of the singer. Evidently this position in no way affects these influences upon listeners (though Murray is very responsive and would be affected more than an average listener wherever he sat).

As I dictate, I reverently become aware that in this present special circumstance Our Blessed Lady is deigning to bestow and produce in our Egos the realization of her wondrous existence. I feel that I may safely say that, according to degrees of responsiveness, these same effects will be produced upon all performers and hearers of this wonderful song, always allowing of course, for strong negative attitudes about religion itself and Our Lady. These obstructive attitudes would be in the personal aura, almost creating a negative response, although no one would be entirely unresponsive.

Repeat Performance

When Wendy Dixon sings "Ave Maria" about three weeks later, I am able to confirm the effects on the performer, es-

82

pecially on the etheric double and the health aura. Radiations from the etheric double almost immediately increase from some three or four inches to about six or eight inches. At the high notes the "antler" effects are very noticeable. The heart chakram, which I may have missed noticing before, almost immediately opens to twice the normal size, glowing golden with an inner core to a funnel of energy from above. I also notice an increased response in the astro-etheric aura, which becomes immediately observable when she begins singing.

I ask Wendy if she is in the same psychological condition as last time. She explains that the previous morning she was elevated to Knighthood in the Round Table, a ceremonial order. The effect is at once observable, though I initially regarded this as only an increased response from psychological change.

When she sings the first verse the "antler" effect appears. Her crown and brow chakras are much increased since the last visit, extending at least twice as far into the astro-mental atmosphere. The throat chakram also is increased, and a certain measure of Kundalini has definitely been safely aroused. It will, if rightly used, deepen her mystical awareness and influence the spiritual effects upon the singer and her audiences.

During the singing gold shines all about her aura, along with a soft though brilliant grass-green from heart to ears. Above that, in various and changing positions, the pure Madonna blue is visible, all of these shining, somewhat blended in the rest of the aura. A beautiful blue Deva flashes into view on her left side some four feet away and remains during the singing, with its attention focused upon her as an individual and at the same time in some way increasing all the above-mentioned effects.

83

As I watch, blue and green appear in the song-ribbon, then yellow on a high note, then blue again. The song-ribbon emanates from the mouth and consists of connected forms, elongated or not according to the length of the note, "ia" of the "Maria" being specially observable, though all are connected.

As the total song is repeated, at least two differing motions of the song-ribbon appear. During the opening line one tends to go from the vocal organs right out from the singer, waving up and down but in no sense losing potency. This outward-going effect keeps recurring. Also, at certain periods the song-ribbon moves in graceful curves throughout the music form and even around the singer. At certain points for some reason it moves forward again, and again passes in and through and about the aura and song form. The song-ribbon and the general music or song form are distinct at all times during the performance, even though the song-ribbon keeps intertwining.

Played upon the Cello

As the melodic lines are played, the whole arm, the bow, and string, are "thrown" into etheric and possibly astral response. The etheric double of the arm increases in size by two inches and the bow by one inch all round. This gives the impression that they are not only vibrant but curiously alive.

I especially note the effects on the etheric double of the wood of the instrument, from the surface of which very fine radiations reach out at least two inches. While the sound and its effects are obviously reaching areas behind the performer, the main stream of music forces emanates from the front of the instrument.

The actual song-ribbon, in its turn, appears to maintain continuity in ovals, spheres, and variously elongated sound forms, all connected while the playing lasts. During pauses, the song-ribbon becomes dissociated and floats off, mostly to the right of the performer and the general music form.

A further striking effect seems to be that, while the radiated sound affects the astro-mental matter in colors corresponding to the notes, a result is produced also at the mental and higher mental levels. Those listeners who are responsive would have awakened and even increased the capacity for meditative and religious thoughts and aspirations. This music is therefore found to have a definite beneficent meditative influence, a spiritualizing effect, upon mind and heart, according to the listener's responsiveness.

As the music continues, I observe that it attracts the attention of members of the angelic hosts, suggesting angelic consciousness attuned to the concept of the great being referred to as the World Mother, Our Blessed Lady. As the music continues at those higher levels, the wonderfully radiant blue of the World Mother's aura becomes evident, as does the presence of lofty angels of similar hue. I find that their interest is directed more towards the pure music and to the composer's and performer's intent rather than to the performer and the audience, and largely limited to the mental and spiritual worlds. The possibility must not be ruled out, however, that individuals, especially women in grave difficulties or prospective mothers, could receive the help of these angelic beings.

This music, I presume, is a link between the inner and outer worlds and therefore a truly spiritual performance. I have no opportunity of judging to what extent the Ego and mental attitude of the performer would affect the response of angelic hosts. There could be no better therapy for a woman in sickness, sorrow, or other need, than the performance of such music as this beautiful "Ave Maria," though as always the effectiveness would depend largely upon the attitude of mind and interior capacity of the performer.

14

"Songs My Mother Taught Me"

Dvorak

This is No. 4 of the "Gypsy Songs" by Dvorak. Wendy Dixon sang, while Hugh and Rae Dixon shared the rather difficult accompaniment on the piano.

> Songs my mother taught me
> In the days long vanished.
> Seldom from her eyelids
> Were the tear-drops banish'd.
>
> Now I teach my children
> Each melodious measure;
> Oft the tears are flowing.
> Oft they flow from my mem'ry's treasure.

I am impressed by the power of certain music (as well as its effects and influence) to evoke the memories imprinted in the akashic record.[1] When music with a past that is well established is performed, it awakens the occult observer to the akashic imprint or memory of nature associated with the

------

1. The Akasha (Sanskrit) is an all-pervading, nonphysical medium or subtle fluid that sustains vibrations of the nature of sound. The akashic record is the repository of nature's memory of events.

87

music. In this case, apart from the musical performance, a kind of tribal gypsy performance is going on in the garden and beyond.

Outside the house and behind the window I observe almost wild dancing which is not represented in the music at all. This seems to have some relationship with a huge occult akashic tribe associated with the life of brilliantly clad dancers, now whirling and flowing around. A dozen or so of them are having a wonderful time, chanting and calling out as they dance. This relates to the memory of the music.

Evidently old music has a memory, and playing it evokes some of that memory in the akasha surrounding the performance, causing it to reproduce some of the original imprint. This is very important, not so much in this case, but in deeply spiritual and "occultly" spiritual music, some of which is very ancient. When performed, such music reproduces in the akasha some of the incidents and atmosphere of the original. I presume that religious music, old hymns, and chants all have their akashic effects too.

15

"Agnus Dei"

Plainsong Chant

This is a Plainsong chant which Murray Stentiford and Hugh Dixon sang in organum: that is, the chant was sung by the two voices in unison but five notes apart (at the interval of a perfect fifth), re-enacting the style of early sacred music.

The first very noticeable effects that strike me are that both singers produce a vertical stream of thought-sound directly as a continuation of their bodies. This stream rises high above the roof of our home—one of the personal results of this chanting. The room is filled with colored music effects which flow off from the voices and heads and bodies of the singers down to their shoulders. The colors include a very beautiful soft leaf-green flowing off from the right side and the arms, out into the room and beyond, enlarging and spreading as it extends far beyond the wall of the house.

This streaming flow of sound effect of great beauty is followed by a roseate glow which seems to establish itself within the large green stream. Thereafter, an aura of gold and yellow shines around the heads of the singers, extending somewhat further into the room as the chanting draws to a close. The color—a beautiful rose—is the color of divine love, beyond my power adequately to describe.

These effects are produced in the auras of both singers. I presume the upshooting vertical force is offered to the "Agnus Dei"[1] from within their inner selves by the full understanding of the Latin words of the title. The main color in the room now after this further chanting—a color we do not have in the physical world—is a blend of extremely delicate, interiorly-lighted pure blue with a roseate hue, also interiorly lighted. These blended together produce a most wonderful wine-like coloring—really glorious. Forces fly off also from the lower part of the bodies of both singers, more or less parallel to the surface of the earth. This lateral influence is specially noticeable as it reaches my own aura. Thus there are at least four main colors produced by the chanting: leaf-green at the beginning, blue and rose interblended into an indescribably beautiful radiance, and then a golden yellow.

As far as I observe at present, there is no powerful force manifesting as in some of the other music. Hitherto, this energy has been very great and is observed as pouring out from an interior source. During the present performance any such force emanates very gently, a curious phenomenon to me as the observer.

Some time after the singing ceases, I become aware of the presence and attention of an order of Devas almost entirely of the same shade of blue that had been observed in the astro-mental atmosphere of the room. They also are chanting, notably at the higher mental and upper subplanes of the formal mental level, and not much lower. One angel is attracted almost immediately by the chanting. It is located some forty or fifty feet up in the air, a little to the right of one of the singers. In some way this particular chant is related to this angel and the order of Ghandarvas or music angels to which

---

1. *Agnus Dei* (Latin), "Lamb of God," a reference to the Lord Jesus Christ.

18 "Agnus Dei," Plainsong Chant

it belongs. The work of this order is almost entirely devotional, having been associated with such music in ancient days.

An Ancient Cathedral

I find myself now in a great old cathedral with this particular Deva and orders of Devas. [18] I am there now in the choir with the altar fully illumined in form on the mental plane as a wonderful atmosphere which surrounds all of us in the cathedral. A human choir is also chanting, and these great Devas are responding to that wonderful choral effort. The altar itself is aglow with golden light and the chanting is proceeding wonderfully.

The cathedral is almost full, and now I see that this particular Deva and accompanying small group are present-day evoked representatives of the order of angels associated with this kind of music. (See illustration.) The current chanting has linked us in time with the *akashic* records. In one sense I am now seated in this glorious ancient cathedral with its full congregation somewhere in Central Europe, possibly southern Germany. This work "Agnus Dei," was chanted and sung by the choir, which was a very large one with some elderly singers, some deep voices, along with the choir boys on either side of the aisle.

This is a wonderful occasion with which I am privileged thus to have been linked at the time when this particular chant was included in the congregational experience.

Now, as I withdraw my attention deliberately from such an inspiring and entirely new experience, it seems evident that music which has sound form and intention links us with the past and in some way evokes in the Akasha a reappearance of the scenes in which that ancient music was once performed.

16

"Greensleeves"

Traditional Melody

This traditional melody was popular in the days of Henry VIII. Shakespeare made reference to "Greensleeves" twice in his play *The Merry Wives of Windsor* (Act II, Sc. I and Act V Sc. 5). It is difficult to trace its original form, but in the version here performed the tune is distinctly modal in character—in fact in the Dorian Mode (utilizing a scale from D to D on the white notes of a piano).

In the first performance the singer was accompanied by an ensemble of piano, clarinet, trumpet, and horn. The music was specially arranged by Michael Dixon for the odd combination of available instruments.

The performers were Wendy Dixon (soprano), Murray Stentiford (clarinet), Hugh Dixon (trumpet), Michael Dixon (horn) and Rae Dixon (piano).

———

In the air and superphysically the first verse produces a wave-like motion from each instrument and player, thereafter extending far beyond the house. [19] The main colors are green and buttercup yellow, the latter waving and flowing out as they play. It is also apparent at shoulder level and extends upwards beyond walls and ceiling, further and further as the music continues. In addition, a golden rosette in the region of the performers' heads spreads like a widening nimbus. Still beyond, there are green and white outflowings in this beautiful soft, waving movement.

Devas and nature spirits are strongly attracted. [19] As I watch an Earth Deva and nature spirits which I can only refer to as the "spirits of the earth" respond from well below ground level. The Deva pauses as if listening, then draws nearer to a distance of about a hundred feet, then nearer again, until it comes almost to the feet of the performers, all the while remaining impersonal to the last degree.

Other outflowing forces are radiating from the head and shoulders of the singer in all directions, and her aura shines with yellow where the heart would be, and green beyond. The very beautiful Earth Deva is, I note, accompanied by many dancing nature spirits from the garden who are affected by the music and remain in the room.

Upon repetition of the first verse, the throat chakras of the standing performers are now thrown into supernormal activity, spinning more rapidly, widening from their throats and extending beyond the sheets of music in their hands—a very remarkable effect. Also from deep down in the earth an uprush of earth force comes up through the legs and spines of the performers and shoots out of their heads, stirring the brow and crown chakras into heightened activity. This should heighten the general awareness of the performers, especially towards the beauty and influence of nature. The singer's heart is answering widely to this effect, increasing in size and activity with a lovely sky blue and yellow rosette. This betokens a glorious flower-like expansion of the heart as a center of the highest emotions, as well as a manifestation of expansion of the chakram.

19 *"Greensleeves," Traditional Melody*

Light-hearted though the music seems, it is really connected with the inner spirit of nature at the mineral and soil level, up through the plant kingdom and into the air, evoking responses from nature as it is performed. A delightful experience both physically and superphysically.

With the next repetition effects round the knees and feet and in the room now show a considerable measure of deep purple just evoked and joining the general aura of the room. A host of air nature spirits or sylphs and an individualized Air Deva, an advanced being, are attracted by the performance. The aura of the angel envelops the room and us, reaching above the roof, imparting a mystic identity with those present, and very responsive to the spirit of "Greensleeves." This piece is powerfully evocative of Devas and nature spirits, of Air and Earth particularly.

The effect of the music itself seems to be in waves with the wave-like movement from each performer timed to the rhythm of the work. Performing together evokes a degree of unity and an inner relationship among the performers.

Now the music has stopped and the auras of the standing performers have become pervaded by that same purple color and are much quickened and extended.

"Greensleeves" is now played on the piano. The song-ribbon is clearly apparent and in accordance with previous descriptions as to shape and elongation according to note, whether connected with particular notes or not. Blue, yellow, and green are again very noticeable, the ribbon itself emanating from the piano and floating around the room. This effect is still faintly present two minutes later, though as time passes each note form loses color and shape and eventually dissipates as the effect no longer influences astro-mental matter.

Now accompanied only by the piano, the singer sings "Greensleeves" in its entirety. I note that her health aura extends at least twelve inches all around her body, and the etheric double is also responsive. The high notes cause an upshooting from the heart region, through the throat, and out through the crown, in a shaft of light extending for six or more feet. This, I notice, is distinct from sound-ribbons.

The performer's astro-mental aura increases in size. Yellow plays in and around the left side of the aura. On her right side is yellow, with green nearest the body, increasing in the aura as she sings. Interestingly, the shape of the body becomes to some extent reproduced in double size in the astro-mental counterpart of the body, and then again beyond that.[1] An effect like auric "antlers" rises on either side above her temples and spreads out over the head for about two feet, so that while she sings she somehow reproduces in the subtle body the graceful beauty of the deer. In this performer the Kundalini force arises and flows up the spine and out the top of the head.

---

1. In addition to the ovoid-shaped aura, clairvoyants report a counterpart or duplicate of the physical body at the astral and mental levels. See C. W. Leadbeater, *Man Visible and Invisible,* Chapter XIV. (Ed.)

17

"Londonderry Air"

Traditional Irish Melody

The true name of this traditional Irish melody from County Derry is "In Derry Vale." It is sung unaccompanied by Wendy Dixon.

In Derry Vale beside the singing river,
So oft I strayed, ah, many years ago,
And culled at morn the golden daffodillies
That came with Spring to set the world aglow.
Oh Derry Vale my thoughts are ever turning
To your broad stream and fairy-circled lea,
For your green isles my exiled heart is yearning,
So far away across the sea.

In Derry Vale amid the Foyle's dark waters
The salmon leap above the singing weir,
The seabirds call—I still can hear them calling
In night's fond dreams of those so dear.
Oh tarrying years, fly faster, ever faster,
I long to see the vale belov'd so well.
I long to know that I am not forgotten
And there at home in peace to dwell.

20 *"Londonderry Air," Traditional Irish Melody*

At once I note that the music song-ribbon consists of a series of forms all in the same ribbon-connection, extending right out of the window and into the gardens beyond. The fundamental color (allowing for individual note changes) is a special form of green, rather like rushes or perhaps, if I may say so, asparagus! There is also an undercurrent of blue.

Extending beyond, a golden radiance shines out and within this green-blue music form—a most wonderful roseate glow, again with yellow at the heart. [20] If I were looking into this distinctly flower-like example of the song alone, then the petals would be described as mostly golden yellow, radiant with an aura extending far beyond themselves in the subtler worlds of colors—a tremendous effect.

In the interior flower-like form itself, the petals are mainly golden yellow. Outwards and inwards from their sides radiations of sound-energy are visible in various colors (notably rose and blue) and stretch several feet beyond the petal forms. Within, there is a highly complex interplay of colored forces and, strangely, their arrangement suggests *the inside* of a flower *within* the petals of the wonderful central forms seen there.

As the first verse is sung completely, the music form "goes waving" out beyond the window, continuing to flow as a wondrous song-ribbon and eventually dissipating into the air beyond.

I suggest (unscientific though this may sound) that something resembling an echo from a supposed aerial sounding-board (as far as, or farther away than, the walls of the next house) returns a softer and smaller song-ribbon running along the ground and connecting again with the source—the singer. The song-ribbon is wave-like, down a little, up a little, and rises in wave-like forms. I cannot say whether the highest note is at the highest position on this wave; I will watch to see if it is a question of the note. But the beautiful, regular, wave-like form is one of the lovely astro-mental characteristics of this artist's singing.

Green and gold in flower-like form, as I have described, pulsates with great activity, extending down to the interior of the flower. A gold and green ribbon connects all the forms at this point, especially the green and gold.

As the sound continues, the form goes out, spreading as it goes into a large beautiful flower form, unlike any known flower. I think there must be a geometrical governing principle at work because the petals are so clearly shaped by processes unknown to me. It seems that the words produce the flower-like effect in the astro-mental air.

As the second verse is sung, I confirm the rhythmic wave-like motions shaped by the flow of connected sound forms, the higher notes producing the upper peaks of the waves, the lower ones sweeping down, and the whole pattern flowing on in the lovely wave-like form largely corresponding (I presume) to the music and the notes.

The second verse is sung again. The experience is truly wonderful, and I cannot but be impressed by the shape in which the component song forms appear, and in their variations. There is one in which the "flower petals" are pointed, while with others they are rounded a little. I notice distinct changes of color with every note, but it is sometimes beyond my capacity to say which note produces which color. Some of the music forms, particularly smaller ones, are predominantly purple. I notice the appearance of music and note forms which have no connection with the ribbon but appear almost explosive and then disappear within the singer's aura.

Interestingly, the effect on the singer varies on her left side. I observe phenomena associated with the garden, grass, orchard, and down beyond the house on the singer's left. Her aura contains what I can only describe as a kind of playful grouping of similar forms which has attracted certain nature spirits who are jumping and dancing on her left, and also in the room and on the ground. They are chiefly Air spirits, sylphs. Some are attracted by the beautiful singing music form, by the activity going on within it, and also by the psychological states of the singer. These are natural denizens of air, radiant creatures, all gold, all blue, and so on. They are small, very lovely little creatures. They are all winged—that is to say their little auras flow in wing-like shapes. Curiously, there is one that is blue; it has just flown in front of me, a beautiful all-blue sylph. It is bent half back as I see it. They are all moving in graceful dances within the aura of the singer. Her aura and personality are much quickened and clarified by the singing and by association with the nature spirits. Either in a former life, or earlier in this one, the singer has, I assume, made links with the four Elements (Earth, Air, Fire and Water) and their associated spirits and Devas of the angel kingdom.

With further singing, I now more closely observe that, in addition to the song-ribbon, the singing and the music fill the room with active forces and beautiful soft colors, especially from the throat and lips of the singer. These assume wide hemispherical form filled with color and light, which are filled with the results of the music itself. This pervading influence produces the colors purple, gold, green, yellow, and blue. The singer is, in consequence, in the midst of these influences of the music, although they are chiefly noticeable in front of her and going right out of the room and for many yards into the air.

102

The "circumference" of the great "song hemisphere" is at first the size of the vocal organs, but almost immediately stretches around to form the side of a great bowl filled with the sound effects. The edges, particularly the upper ones, vary with the note in both color and shape; the top notes send up a high roof or V-shaped extension, while the other notes form "musical nodules" on the surface, varying in size and color according to the note. The whole room is filled with this particular pattern which is entirely unaffected by physical substance and extends above the ceiling, below the floor, and out.

Investigating the effect of the music upon the audience, I note a phenomenon I have never before noticed. Within the "bowl," in addition to a ribbon of music forms produced by word and note, there is emitted also a flow of unformed energy that streams straight out from the voice for varying distances. This song-stream, distinct from the ribbon-forms, is emitted directly forward and continues to exist in length and size according to the length and volume of the note. The longer the note, the longer the stream continues. With some of the notes the stream goes out of the room, others halfway, while some remain near to the singer, a few yards in front, and then fade into the general form. All are correctly colored according to the note, notably blue and gold.

Thus I discover there are not only sound-ribbons, each with linked sound forms, but there are also streams for each word, note, or group of notes, outflowing from the vocal organs directly ahead of the singer who is following the available text.

One may thus presume that the shape of the mouth and position of the lips of performers are not only responsible for the song-ribbon *forms*, but that this "energy-stream" flows

103

out through the lips into the air. Vocal organs and mouth may be likened to a generating instrument, and as the singing continues each note generates power which is directed outwards in the three forms—the appropriately colored song-ribbon, the air-filled "bowl," and the song streams.

18

Prelude in C Sharp Minor

J. S. Bach

Bach's music exemplifies his deep religious aspirations. This is evident not only in his mighty works for chorus and orchestra, but also in his music for keyboard alone. This prelude is No. 4 in Book I of the 48 Preludes and Fugues by J. S. Bach. It is played on the piano by Murray Stentiford.

As I observe the effects of this wonderful piece of music, I find my mind elevated, however slightly, towards the divine Creator and, however partially, to the divine processes of Creation. Apart from the lovely music forms which were described in my book *Music Forms* and which extend so beautifully all over the room, the effects upon the performer and upon all responsive listeners would be to attune the personality, particularly the mind, more and more closely into harmony with the inner Self. This applies especially with regard to the ordered harmony of the universe and the laws under which it finds expression throughout the planes of nature. Thus one realizes, however incompletely, the interior, indwelling spiritual Being, the One Alone, who conceives of worlds and universes, and who in musical terms utters a sound containing notes and chords expressive of *part* of the Great Word, including the whole concept of the deific consciousness of the universe.

This realization needs to be gradually transferred, plane by plane, from those spiritual heights, through Atma (spiritual will), Buddhi (spiritual wisdom-intuition), and the higher Manas (intelligence), into the formal mind where this great work would seem to express the God-pattern with which it is wholly in tune.

The player's mental body responds wonderfully, especially from the shoulders upwards, so that while playing, his consciousness is associated with the divine composite Word, and the whole mind-brain becomes increasingly attuned to, one with, and expressive of an aspect of the One Word.[1]

The player's astro-mental aura is extended considerably and set in motion by the rhythm and successive patterns of those different colored portions of the music form according to the phases through which the mind and emotions are passing.

The astral and mental bodies have now both been expanded to a distance of some six or eight feet from the neck and shoulders. As I endeavor to observe, these become curiously formulated like waves, groups of modulated hills and dales, all linked in continuing pattern expressive of one concept of the Divine. This process continues.

As occurs also in meditation, the center of the brain is stimulated to a greater sensitivity of Egoic consciousness. The thalamus and hypothalamus in the center of the head

---

1. The One Word: In the beginning was the Word, and the Word was with God, and the Word was God. St. John 1:1.

are stimulated. The sound effects continue in them and in the texture and molecules of that part of the brain and associated organs. All these have been set vibrating at a rate more rapid and therefore more receptive than usual.

This composition is clearly a meditative work and, I would suggest, is very *beneficial* indeed.

19

"Our Worship Rises Like a Soaring Flame"

Anonymous Tune

The words of this hymn are written by the Reverend C. W. Scott-Moncrieff. They are sung to the tune "St. Charles" (anon.), by Wendy Dixon accompanied by Rae Dixon on the piano.

A music form is built within the vocal organs of the singer as if a root and stalk were there. Emerging from the mouth, this opens out in a beautiful, ever-enlarging flower form, the whole alternating between an uneven enlargement and a slight reduction, until it extends about fifteen yards. [21] Within its enclosing limits, it is full of green, blue, and gold flickering amid the smoothly outflowing, though slightly wavering, total form. This, I assume, will continue extending and enlarging as the singing continues. (Later this is confirmed.) That is the first effect.

Within the outer form is a more regular outpouring form, flower-like and opening, showing violet mingling with the other colors. From the beginning at the heart is a shape that resembles a small bulb.

As three continuous verses are sung, the vocal music form spreads farther and farther beyond the singer. After

21 *"Our Worship Rises Like a Soaring Flame," Anonymous Tune*

the third verse the distance has reached at least twenty feet. I must mention that the forms constantly produced move *within themselves* in small undulations, with the exception of the central figure and immediate areas which resemble the heart of a wondrous flower. This central portion begins as a small globular form of many colors, especially gold and violet, and then expands, reaching the extent of the containing form. It keeps changing in shape according to the words and notes. Violet is noticeable, especially within the beautiful flower shape with its ever-moving external enclosure and changing internal developments.

I now see and learn that hymn singing, especially with such beautiful and inspiring words, also has a profound effect upon a sensitive and mystically inclined performer, depending almost entirely upon the degree to which the occult forces in the physical and superphysical bodies had previously been aroused. The effect is almost immediate, causing the singer's aura to expand and become illumined around the head and shoulders in response to the radiations of the immortal self and the elevating music.

Thus, I see further wonderful benefits accruing to all singers of uplifting sacred songs, especially psalms and hymns; for these attract the inner Self into increasingly close relationship with the outer person. When the subject is sufficiently responsive, expansions of consciousness, elevations of religious thought, and even realizations thereof, can occur. Congregations might well be informed of this, so that responsive ones could benefit from heightened consciousness while singing. This surely is very important, since the effects could operate throughout the life of the individual. The value of ecclesiastical music and its performance singly or by groups would be increased by such understanding of the songs.

As I listen and watch, the thought comes strongly to me—and I venture to repeat it—that the organist could contribute greatly if trained to work consciously for the general upliftment while accompanying. Organists have a wonderful opportunity for such training should they be interested. This of course applies even more to choirs, for if a whole choir were singing with these intents, the effects upon each member, the clergy, and the congregation could be greatly increased. Thus viewed, church worship could become even more elevating and produce greater effects upon consciousness than are now evident.

As the piece is repeated I realize another aspect of the superphysical effects of this music which I want to confirm. I wish to concentrate on this particular hymn which refers to the angels themselves and see if I have missed anything. I find (as I should have known) that the accent is upon the divinity of the universe, especially upon the Second Aspect as incarnate in the Lord Jesus Christ, referred to as "Master." As that word is uttered, an increased response from the Master occurs. Within the form already described there flows through the head and vocal organs of the singer a flood of golden-yellow light, illuminating and irradiating the form. Angels *did* respond at the first verse. They appeared to me to be First Ray,[1] or I may have been misled by their shape caused by the upward flow of their auras from shoulders and above (where the head would be), which I can only describe as crown-like.

As I observe and thus record, an angel "speaks" to me somewhat as follows: "We are not First Ray but members of that hierarchy concerned with the emanation of the divine

1. See my book *The Seven Human Temperaments* (Adyar: Theosophical Publishing House, 1981).

111

Idea of the universe, and with our subordinates we build all forms according to the Word. It is chiefly the angels of music who respond. Within reasonably developed humanity there is a spiritual capacity which can best be described as adoration, which is one of the highest, noblest, and most spiritual of human capacities. This hymn evokes that quality in the singer and would do so in congregations. Though associated with such a chant because of its opening verses, we are not participating in the performance."

The cherubs are all around us as we listen. These are beautiful little nature spirits of varying development with angelically child-like faces, with wings from the shoulders but little else in the construction of their forms. They fly around rejoicing and appear to be singing, with their mouths opening and closing. Thus I assume that there does exist an order of angelic hosts different from anything I have before experienced. I presume that they are the younger members of a hierarchy of the music angels, which are concerned with the whole divine art of music (even of nature herself and her songsters) and all human musicians, and right up to the highly evolved order of angels called by the Hindus "Ghandarvas."

I recognize a certain highly spiritual and extremely important aspect—the significance and function of the art of music. This *might* perhaps be described as an expression of the Logoic song, the exalted divine manifestation of the one timeless Idea of the universe throughout its evolution. The Divine Musician is far beyond the limitations of any separate order of music or kinds of instruments and voices, being the purely divine aspect of music.

20

The Prince of Denmark March

Jeremiah Clarke

This popular piece from the trumpet repertoire is often referred to as the "Trumpet Voluntary" and commonly attributed to Henry Purcell. However, authority now attributes it to Jeremiah Clarke, who was a contemporary of Purcell.

It is interesting to note that Geoffrey Hodson discerned the aspect of kingliness *before* knowing the title of the piece. The work was played on the trumpet by Hugh Dixon, accompanied on the piano by Murray Stentiford.

I am at once impressed by the astro-mental effects of the music which reach out beyond the walls of this house towards the one next door. This is the first thing that strikes me—the extended range of the mento-astral effects of sound.

As the music is played, the effects on the players are noticeable, for the Kundalini or creative energy is aroused, shooting up their spines and out of the tops of their heads high into the air. For a conscious and awakened occultist, this would assist greatly in producing occult effects.

One of the main colors, which fill the room and extend far above and around, is the highest, golden yellow. [22] Also, green appears at the level of the trumpet itself and reaches down to the knees in varying and darkening shades. This shows first as waves and movements in the colors in the air, causing the upper half of the whole music form to ripple as if it became changed into small wavelets every time the appropriate trill is played. As stated, the effect upon the player remains strong, especially on the back. This could benefit the nerves of the body which extend from the back, and the effect would act generally as an energizer to a responsive person, certainly being very stimulating.

Although, as now, the playing has temporarily stopped, this effect passes round the head as a growing "halo." It is divided fairly equally into colors of purple by the throat and heart, yellow or golden at the instrument, and green above, plus violet produced in the upper areas by this music. This continues in the player's aura, but gradually fades throughout the room.

As the performance is repeated, radiations of gold shoot out from behind the performer's head into the astro-mental atmosphere. At the same time the trills are remarkable, starting within the instrument and rising above and a little forward and away from the performer, causing small wavelets in the "form" of the music-essence and effects that increasingly surround the performer. These, and the whole music form, reach forty or fifty feet into the air. The whole astro-mental surroundings respond to the vibratory effects, glowing with the many colors, much as I have described.

From the bell of the trumpet itself, widening as if from a funnel, a stream of brightly colored power concentrates and maintains the funnel in front of the performer. During the performance he is surrounded by wave-like changes in the astro-mental atmosphere, reaching beyond the house for hundreds of yards and high into the air.

22 The Prince of Denmark *March, Jeremiah Clarke*

As far as I can now see, this wave-like rising sound effect is also present with the other influences shooting, shining, flashing, and flowing through it. There is, for example, a special effect produced behind the performer's neck, and a pale lavender force also emanates from the bronchial tubes. Studying this, I observe a curious disturbance in the performer's astro-mental aura—a very beautiful lavender from neck and shoulders and reaching behind him for some two feet.

Studying the effects upon the audience, I note that the opening bars produce a shock, and I see in her aura that one person is startled. This response begins with a kind of stimulating shock which causes the health aura to expand, and the etheric double to heighten and speed up its vibration, insofar as it is able, thereby increasing the intake of prana or vital energy.

Astrally, it is as if a strong wind blows the etheric double of the performers and listeners slightly and the astro-mental strongly, thereby causing the auras to spread out in the same wave-like movement. The inherent musical sense gradually replaces the shock with enjoyment and responsiveness to the beauty of the music. This affects the auras of all present (chiefly from the elbows upwards), expanding them and causing the inner selves to become more attentive to the personalities and also to listen to the lovely music in what could be described as a mystical experience. The performance thus brings the Ego into closer relationship with the personality.

Deep within the middle of the head and corresponding regions, there is a state of consciousness which I can only describe as "religious appreciation," or even as "worship of beautiful music." The listeners' etheric doubles, I observe,

116

are stretched beyond normal, extending even from six to nine inches, while the astro-mental auras are still more greatly stimulated. This may be true of all "good" music, but it is very noticeable during the present performance.

There is, I note, an almost immediate response from an order of Ghandarvas. I may almost describe them as "divine trumpeters." One of them is golden yellow, while behind and above it there shines a "choir" of archangelic sound reproducers. This order of Devas exists at supramental levels and, if I am correct, seems to be instinct with the spiritual and even personal ideal of royalty, a principle which exists within the consciousness of the great beings "behind" human existence. This supramental influence affects those present who are able to respond by stimulating their evolutionary development, notably that inner spirituality which could be named "kingliness," that First Ray quality, and the truly royal capacity to control the personality, a valuable aspect of this performance.

The kingly "trumpet" angels evoked by the performance belong to the hierarchy of First Ray Deva Rajas and Devas of the sevenfold outpoured creative power of the Solar Logos. They function under a great archangel king of our planet. They have glorious crown-like upward radiations above the head which give a wonderfully regal appearance, the whole being richly colored.

21

Horn Concerto No. 1

Haydn

The second or slow movement of this concerto written for horn and strings is in the key of A major, and its long, singing phrases call for all the sustained beauty of tone of which the horn is capable, both in the higher and the dark lower registers. It is played by Michael Dixon, unaccompanied.

At once I perceive a fairly concentrated central stream of colored energy surrounded by a widely opening funnel-shaped stream. [23] This stream is not made up of only a single color according to note, as I expected; the predominating colors include also red, green, and yellow, all merged with the major note coloring. This, I think, results from an "echo effect" produced by the metal of the instrument vibrating at different speeds round the bell shape of the horn.

Thus, while the main sound form emanates from the end of the instrument and primarily travels in that direction, strangely, the whole instrument sends out color-producing music energies. Indeed the whole instrument is highly contributive to the superphysical effect upon both the performer and all around him. However these colors and their "vibrations" are utterly different in appearance from those of singing. Actually the whole effect is like an exceedingly fine

23 *Horn Concerto no. 1, Haydn*

tremolo, not in the ordinary usage of that term, but as a marvelously fine-tooth-comb-like vibration.

As the next phrase is played, the song-ribbon spreads throughout and beyond the room, unlike the singing of "Ave Maria" and certain other works, for here the song-ribbon flows out into the hall and beyond, even passing out of the house. The other effects are primarily produced *within* the aura of the performer and around him in continually varying, highly trembling, colored music energy. The song-ribbon and its effects extend increasingly as the performance continues, and therefore they quickly reach out far beyond the house.

In the next phrase I notice that each of the first group of notes produces a separate (or not) interconnected sequence of sound forms, chiefly red, green, yellow, I presume according to its specific note color. The first ones are mostly spherical and surrounded by a radiation as they float out from the instrument. Many of these rise above the performer's head; all emanate out the end of the horn, some not lasting very long.

I note that the general effect of this stage resembles the sudden appearance in the astro-mental "air" of a succession of sound forms which are not quite spherical but rather ovoid shaped. Some of these, particularly those from short and quavering notes, arise above and around the performer's head. Many seem almost as if dancing in the air above him and then vanish, doubtless when the sound effects of the physical notes (almost staccato) come to an end. At least the phenomenon thus seems to me.

Now the room has become full of those sound forms, while the song-ribbon components, many of which are interconnected, become a continuing stream. Almost all of these components are shaped like very elongated ovoids. These are not wholly ovoid, however, but present rather an out-stretched tubular appearance, each with its basic color. Curiously, with this instrument (the horn) if I am observing correctly, there also seems to be a combination of the blended colors, chiefly in the outer third or quarter of the circumference of the song-ribbon form. Many of these play and dance in the air all around the performer and the room and are quite dazzling to watch. They do not appear to last very much longer than the actual sound itself.

A bass passage is now being played, followed by a prolongation of the last note by itself, and it now seems curiously as if, with the instrument thus held, the whole body of the performer is in some way involved, becoming a part of the instrument, at least from the astro-mental point of view. Consequently, some of the musical effects and the radiated etheric forces flow out or are emitted through the body and skin of the shoulders and much of the back of the performer. This differs from the effects of the recently studied singing in which the solar plexus, heart, throat, and brow chakras were all involved in the emission of the music, even though in some cases the voice is the actual producer. From this I am led to the view that the horn or human organs, throat and mouth for example, are not the sole producers of the super-physical effects of the music. Rather, mysteriously, the whole being of the performer, physical, astral, and mental, is included in the performance, presumably varying with her or his psychology and approach to music.

The trills on the long notes are immediately noticeable in the music form, which itself is of a long cylindrical shape. Whenever there is a trill, the cylindrical form itself trembles accordingly, in addition to and participation in that extremely fine trembling already described. This produces a special effect which I have not had the opportunity to observe before. The music emanating from the instrument, in addition to producing the true note color depending chiefly on the length of the note, seems on this particular instrument to bestow upon those present an extremely fine "high" vibration apparent all through the performance.

As far as I am able to judge, a series of intimately related leaf-like forms are sent out in all directions, but mostly above our room, whence they flow in one large production of combined music-formed "leaves." This form, I notice, is slightly waving as it passes out beyond the house and at least halfway down the garden, some twenty yards or more.

The high notes also produce an upward movement of these forms and, in consequence, the total result becomes complicated in the extreme, even though all was centered and originated at the instrument itself.

Here my attempted description must cease as the leaf and flower shapes intertwine, mingle, and play across the form, which no longer maintains a single appearance.

22

"The Vain Suit"

Brahms

A young man is singing to his lady-love, pleading to be allowed to come in out of the cold. She replies that "if his 'love' is not enough to keep him warm, then he had better go home to bed." A charming song which Wendy Dixon sings in German unaccompanied.

During the first verse the performer's aura is pleasantly disturbed, or rather changed in shape, losing its ovoid form and producing "fireworks" or "soundworks" of different colors—green, blue, white, some blue with rose edges— shooting out from the aura beyond the house. That is mostly the auric effect upon the performer. The song-ribbon cannot easily be described because it is continually broken. The components are somewhat explosive, that is, instead of a rounded, completed form, it is more like a long series of somewhat interconnected flash-shaped forms, chiefly white and blue.[24]

In the second verse each separate group of song forms leaves the singer and moves about the room mostly at the level of and slightly above the head. Thus, the song forms cannot be described quite as a ribbon but rather as a group of song forms dancing about the room, partly in affection and partly in fun. The song phrases and "short ribbons" still remain from the preceding verse.

The effect of the third verse on the singer's aura is largely from the shoulders and arms and above the head as she stands, but it is so profound that it causes ripples throughout the aura, a curious irregularity. A ripple is set up and then the aura becomes relatively quiet, then another ripple, another color, and so on. Most of this auric effect shows from the elbows upwards and outwards, though some of it appears laterally, parallel with the floor, and some slopes somewhat upwards. There is also an upflow out the head and through the crown chakram.

On hearing this verse again, I observe the same general effects, the music form contributions being in different colors, some a bit jagged at the edges and at the ends.

Coming to the fourth verse, the sound forms are mostly as I have already described, shooting about the room and up into the sky, as it were, according to note and formation and, I presume, meaning. Some of them seem to be grouped together in front of the face and throat of the singer and come out from her towards me, but others go in other directions.

The effect of this piece of music on the performer was not deep and did not involve the higher consciousness. In other words, the effect is largely astro-mental, concerned with pleasure in the idea, the singing, and the contribution to the morning. All of these are visible as constant little outflowings from the part of the astro-mental body that lies within the physical and flowing out to the edge of the aura and beyond, all in appropriate colors.

From the aura of the singer as she repeats the last verse there emerge from the shoulders and down to the waist

24 *"The Vain Suit," Brahms*

two somewhat wing-like forms, shallow and waving backward and forward. However light-hearted and even unconcerned the words may sound, actually I can sense and see in the aura these forms which I call "love-wings" waving to and fro. In the first part of the verse I see green, some yellow where the singer's heart is, and some roseate color which is rather beautiful.

23

Pavane

Fauré

Though still used by recent composers such as Fauré and Ravel, the pavane as a form had its real importance in the musical life of three to four hundred years ago when it was used to accompany slow, stately court dances. Its rhythm is majestical and processional. At one time its air was sung by the dancers. This pavane was played unaccompanied on the clarinet by Murray Stentiford.

As the note G above middle C is played, the room fills with astro-mental reactions to the sound vibrations, mainly in green, filling the player's aura and reaching beyond the walls. Thereafter, the green becomes lighter and very refined and the player's crown chakram is stimulated. When the note is repeated, an effect appears in a shade darker than sky blue. Within the aura some rose color shines out and eventually joins the other two colors, these effects extending beyond the walls. As the complete pavane is played, there appears a succession of song-ribbon notes in the usual colors, but with rose and sky blue also.

As the music is repeated, it seems as if the general effects, apart from the song-ribbon, are produced primarily within and from the instrument itself, but at the same time they occur secondarily within the performer, whose aura tends to be enlarged and blended with the more extended multicolored musical effects. Occasionally instead of flowing fairly evenly, the song-ribbon almost jumps into a wave-like pattern, an effect which is confirmed when the whole piece is repeated.

In the song-ribbon the music forms display the color of the note, its shape and length, including the occasional curious little frills at the transition from one note form to the next. Very noticeable are occasional breaks in the ribbon, presumably when the tune momentarily ceases, when there is a tendency for the ribbon to dance up and down instead of flowing evenly. The ribbon flows, forms, and streams round the performer, about the room, and out of sight beyond the house.

The general music form is largely wing-like from both instrument and performer. At first I notice it especially at the left and right sides, and then I realize it is at least four-dimensional, with wing-like radiations flowing in all directions. When the music is smooth, the wings assume a smooth texture with the described colors interblended. By the time the music ends these wing-like shapes stretch beyond the house. When the music is beautifully undulating, this is immediately noticeable in the texture as a kind of ripple going through the wings.

The effect on the performer is first observable as an opening of the crown chakram and an increase of its upward flow above the crown of the head. A certain measure of Serpent Fire or Kundalini flows up the spine and out the top of the head. The health aura becomes enlarged, especially that closest to the skin, the outward-streaming force reaching to three or four inches instead of the normal one inch. All of these effects on the performer continue after the playing has ceased.

The heart chakram is also touched as if the sense of love for music in general, however impersonal, and this piece in particular, is concerned. This may well be more typical of the present performer than of one without his response to life and music. This piece is very beneficial to his health, as noted concerning the health aura, some radiations still extending considerably beyond the normal.

The pavane is a sedate dance. Although unaware of the title of the piece, I notice a tendency of both the performer's aura and the music forms in general to have one main sweepingly curved form with graceful ripples, dance-like in appearance, when that type of rhythm is played. This increased vitality comes from the power of sound, a most potent agency. The whole universe is created by sound. Thus this effect upon the performer does not indicate a loss but an increase of vitality, resulting from the creative power of sound by which the universe was created—the Word.

The human health aura consists of one outward stream of prana extending but a few inches, though increased by the performance. In a reasonably healthy person it also includes somewhat irregular streams of outflowing forms, including some golden prana, for about a yard. Where there is disease or ill health, these emanations are reduced. This suggests the study of the use of music for healing purposes. I practiced such healing for some six and a half years in London, combined with colored lights and other forms of treatment, superphysical and physical.

I notice the player's health aura is still extended fifteen minutes after playing, particularly on the left. Pleasure colors show in the astro-mental body, at first chiefly rose, followed by soft green and some yellow evoked from the listeners, thus showing in his aura as happiness, but not only that.

The yellow in and above the head is also increased by the end of the first passage.

As the second passage is repeated, the music forms in mento-astral matter penetrate and sweep through the listeners' auras, evoking partly colored increases in auric activity according, I presume, to their responsiveness. The song-ribbon seems to stay in and around the performer rather than to enter the listeners' auras, except for those near at hand. I get the impression that the song-ribbon is almost an entity, a being, and one whose almost total responsiveness is concerned with the music itself as performed.

On the other hand, the outward-flowing and astro-mental streams of energy and the forms they tend to make sweep into and through the auras of those within range. In the case of an orchestra, this would be very wide indeed, hundreds of yards in fact, producing a wondrous music form in space.

Thus the effect upon the audience is related to the number of instruments and the volume of sound. The pianissimo effect would not reach very far, I presume. An experimental performance and observation support this view, although in a small room everyone present is fully affected by the softer playing.

The two parts are played again. No Devas were particularly attracted, but this piece set many small Earth and garden nature spirits dancing round the floor, especially on the right of the performer. The order of nature spirits that appears, whether gnome, undine, sylph, or salamander, depends on the type of music.

24

Coriolan Overture

Beethoven

A recording of the lyrical melody from this orchestral work (in C minor, Op. 72) was played for comparison of the effects of live and recorded music.

The main colors produced by this melody are a roseate glow on the outer sides of the music form, golden yellow, and then in the center a current of blue. [25] The whole effect, especially on the outsides, is of beautiful waves of many hues. However, the first effects of the music upon superphysical matter begin with these many-colored waves which immediately spread in an ever-widening stream. In consequence, the whole room becomes quickly filled with music from the radiation from the record player's speaker, the many-colored parts appearing and disappearing as different notes and chords are played.

In the center of this radiated shape there is a funnel of music-force suggesting a beautiful opening fountain, the main color being blue with touches of purple, golden yellow, and a roseate glow continuing towards the outside. While the wave-like form remains visible, the center presents a flower-like effect as if this inner funnel were composed of petals. Other effects consist of flashes of radiance which

131

25 Coriolan *Overture, Beethoven*

shoot forth into the room, the colors and intensity varying according to the nature of the music.

In addition, I observe a central stem to the flower-like form which gradually expands from two to three feet in front of the speaker, and in wave-like petals builds an almost rose-shaped form, also glowing with the colors I have already mentioned.

Such appear to be some of the effects produced by the recording of The Coriolan Overture.

25

"Pie Jesus" from Requiem

Fauré

This is the second and final *recorded* selection played for observation of its effects. This extract from Fauré's Requiem is for boy soprano and orchestra. He sings:

> Pie Jesu, Domine, dona eis requiem;
> dona eis requiem sempiternam.

> Blessed Jesus, O Lord, grant them rest;
> grant them eternal rest.

———————

The music ribbon is complete, being green underneath, yellow on top, and gold in the middle, each note rather flower-like. [26] The second part produces massive forms, somewhat like quadrangular pillars, in similar colors. The music-form flows beautifully, emerging from the machine a little below its level for a few yards then sweeping over our heads in a beautiful winding series of generally connected note forms shaped like an Easter lily. The higher notes are a very faint rose with sky blue underneath and some yellow above, and they continue to float about after the singing ceases. Each contributory sound form differs according (I presume) to length and beat, mostly in length and varying a little in color. As the ribbon emerges, for some reason it flows

26 "Pie Jesus" from Requiem, Fauré

slightly downwards towards the left wall, then rises and floats around in beautiful curves.

Each form has a main color, but strangely blended with it on the outside are the other faintly visible colors that I mentioned: a soft green occasionally, a beautiful sky blue, and at one point a little purple. So the music ribbon is built of forms produced in astral matter by the physical sound. Apart from one or two breaks corresponding to the music, a smoothly undulating line or "tube" of music-sound song-ribbon is produced.

Closer observation reveals a duality of each ribbon component. One part is an outward flowing stream, gold being a dominant color. Surrounding that, like the petals of an Easter lily, are evoked responses in astro-mental matter that seem to enfold the central current, which goes on to the next "ribbon." This connects them all as they wave about the room just above the carpet, over our heads, and round in a beautiful unpatterned design, a marvelous soft green being added at that point. Each part of the ribbon of the music form is a miracle of beauty and complexity as shown by the changing colors, each one varying as the ribbon waves about in response to the sound. Sometimes blue is predominant, sometimes a soft green, and at other times a roseate color shines within.

As the recording is repeated, I note that the shapes vary as if I were in a vast collection of different phenomena. Some of the note forms are nearly closed at the end of the petals, others are half open, and some wide open, as is the last one. These differences of form and color appear in each component of the ribbon, and except where the music stops, all are linked together by a connecting flow of astro-mental

136

matter which resembles a central stream in which the continuing forms are shaped. This last one is still there. Its length is related to the size of the note form; the louder and longer-held notes make larger forms which endure longer than those of short-note singing, giving great variation to the wonderful song-ribbon. Indeed each note and its form in astro-mental matter is an interesting study in itself.

In addition, each note form is now "spraying forward" around the essential connecting stream, forming a series of streamlets of sound-energy which, curiously, at petal length tend to fold over and disappear. I get the impression that these result from sound qualities not necessarily heard, as if each note had its own accompanying superphysical forces, thus not being wholly a single production but very complex. Therefore, there must be added to the shapes already described a variation in the angles formed by the "reaching outwards" of the petals, some straight forward, some half way, and others nearly at right angles, presumably according to note. When the note is held, all these tend to unite, making a funnel or flower-shaped figure. There are tremendous subtleties here. I am half watching, half contemplating, in search of an intuitive understanding as well.

I presume that each physical note has its correspondences in vibrational equity on the other planes of nature, so that when a single note is played and heard, these correspondences in the astro-mental and higher worlds show themselves and contribute to the superphysical music form. Hence the various colors which do not seem to fit the note *alone* are now understood to be reflected correspondences from higher planes, producing the complexity of each note form.

137

An Attending Deva

As the performance begins, a beautiful angelic being appears by the door. I bow instinctively, but have to turn my attention to the music form. Yet I know that the Deva is still there.

I realize that this angel belongs to the order associated with the feminine principle and activities of deity, and of the great official holding the representative office within the angelic hosts, the World Mother. Thus predominant in the aura is the blue so correctly intuited by the great artists as associated with our Blessed Lady Mary.

The central form of the Deva is perhaps eight feet tall, its head and shoulders being surrounded by concentric spheres of differing colors born from outrushing energies. They are golden near the shoulders and head for about a foot, then rose-colored for about six inches, and beyond that what I can describe as blue radiance, with a vertical parting or uprushing from the center of the head, a widening cone-shaped current, mostly lavender and white. This place in the head of the Deva is the center of power. Below that, the colors radiate at right angles through the forehead and heart positions.

The aura of the Deva extends beyond the walls, above the ceiling, and below the floor of the room. One of its functions, I gather, is to project the power (for which it is an agent) into the consciousness and aura of listeners who can respond to the power of the World Mother and the spiritualizing influence of this order of beings. Thus we are in the presence of a ministering angel with feminine distinctiveness, drawn to service by the people and the music, and assisting those responsive to a deeper realization of the compassionate World Mother who, in the thought of the Deva, enfolds all humanity, especially newborn babies and young children.

This system of correspondences between the highest levels of being and lower levels awakens whenever the appropriate forces are liberated in the worlds of form. These were evoked by the consciousness, thought, and intent of the singing and music. I now realize that the title of the song is indicative of this correspondence, which might perhaps be regarded as an effect of music upon listeners. According to their responses and realizations, the listeners are not only quickened in certain areas of their natures but also assisted by angelic beings, especially the Ghandarvas, archangels and angels of sound.

I ask the Deva, "Has any influence of the Lord Jesus been touched?" The Deva answers, "Yes, of course, but he, the Great Adept, is not specially associated with the World Mother principle or with human motherhood as is our Blessed Lady. The Lord Jesus is more fully engaged than could possibly be imagined in the task of his order in relation to the work of the Solar Logos *as a whole.* Consequently, his attention would tend to be drawn towards the condition of devotion to Him."

Question: "Did the Lord Jesus *himself* respond while the music was played, named as it is for him?"

"Yes, but from *within* the listeners, not without, head and heart being revealed, insofar as a listener can respond physically and superphysically." Therefore, if I am correct, the Great Lord responds at the level of the abstract worlds and planes, from the interior rather than externally and objectively.

The World Mother evidently works thus also, using an order of angelic hosts through which to influence and illumine human intelligence and to convey to mankind the spirit of boundless, selfless maternal love and devotion. I conclude that Our Blessed Lady directly and through her order of angels—but in a way different from Our Lord—keeps unbroken contact with the humanity she ever loves and helps. This applies especially where childbirth, children, and parenthood are concerned. As I listen and thus watch, I realize this is only part of her work in ministering to the human kingdom.

To conclude, one of music's effects is to awaken within the hearer corresponding states of consciousness, from coarse up to realms of beauty and truth, according to the ability of the hearer to respond to angelic ministrations. Good music therefore is a wonderful instrument for stimulating awareness in the higher nature, improving and purifying the personality, and increasing spiritual responses.

Music that stimulates the lower side of human nature can be extremely harmful, while religious music, especially that associated with the Lord Jesus and his mother, evokes benediction and angelic response. Other kinds of music stir corresponding responses *within the hearer* from adeptic and angelic agencies. The poet spoke the truth when he said: "Good music is the voice of God speaking to the souls of men."

QUEST BOOKS

Books on related subjects:

BROTHERHOOD OF ANGELS AND MEN—
Geoffrey Hodson
The author receives messages from the angelic
kingdom concerning man's life-style.

THE CHAKRAS— *Charles W. Leadbeater*
With ten color plates, this is a clairvoyant
examination of man's psychic force centers.

DYNAMICS OF THE PSYCHIC WORLD—
Comp. by Lina Psaltis
Excerpts from the writings of H.P. Blavatsky on
magic, mediumship, and our latent spiritual powers.

ETHERIC BODY OF MAN— *Phoebe and Laurence Bendit*
A clairvoyant and a psychiatrist combine
their talents to explore man's aura.

FAIRIES AT WORK AND PLAY— *Geoffrey Hodson*
A detailed description of the life-forces
that surround us and influence our life.

MAN, VISIBLE AND INVISIBLE— *Charles W. Leadbeater*
With twenty-six color paintings
depicting the subtle bodies of man.

THE MIRACLE OF BIRTH— *Geoffrey Hodson*
A clairvoyant description of prenatal life.

THOUGHT FORMS— *Annie Besant & C.W. Leadbeater*
With fifty-eight b/w and full color paintings
of our thought forms as seen clairvoyantly.

Available from:
The Theosophical Publishing House
306 West Geneva Road
Wheaton, Illinois 60189